CW00807308

Let's Be Honest Are You Really Ready for College?

90 Mini-Chapters to Help You Prepare

Adam Barnett

WESTBOW
PRESS®
A DIVISION OF THOMAS NELSON
& ZONDERVAN

Copyright © 2019 Adam Barnett.

All rights reserved. No part of this book may be used or reproduced by any means, graphic, electronic, or mechanical, including photocopying, recording, taping or by any information storage retrieval system without the written permission of the author except in the case of brief quotations embodied in critical articles and reviews.

WestBow Press books may be ordered through booksellers or by contacting:

WestBow Press
A Division of Thomas Nelson & Zondervan
1663 Liberty Drive
Bloomington, IN 47403
www.westbowpress.com
1 (866) 928-1240

Because of the dynamic nature of the Internet, any web addresses or links contained in this book may have changed since publication and may no longer be valid. The views expressed in this work are solely those of the author and do not necessarily reflect the views of the publisher, and the publisher hereby disclaims any responsibility for them.

Any people depicted in stock imagery provided by Getty Images are models, and such images are being used for illustrative purposes only.
Certain stock imagery © Getty Images.

Unless noted otherwise, all Scripture quotations are taken from The Holy Bible, New International Version®, NIV® Copyright © 1973, 1978, 1984, 2011 by Biblica, Inc.® Used by permission. All rights reserved worldwide.

Scripture quotations marked MSG are taken from The Message. Copyright © 1993, 1994, 1995, 1996, 2000, 2001, 2002. Used by permission of NavPress Publishing Group.

Interior Image Credit: Martin Taylor Creative (martintaylor.work)

Editors:
Amy Wopsle (amy@shine-businesssolutions.com)
Kristi Tackett

ISBN: 978-1-9736-7649-2 (sc)
ISBN: 978-1-9736-7650-8 (hc)
ISBN: 978-1-9736-7648-5 (e)

Library of Congress Control Number: 2019915943

Print information available on the last page.

WestBow Press rev. date: 11/1/2019

Endorsements

"'Let's Be Honest... Are you Really Ready for College?' is an outstanding book for teens looking to transition smoothly from high school into a university. Adam Barnett does a phenomenal job at laying out clear expectations of what college will look like and how to prepare for it. The transition from high school to college is one of the most influential seasons in a young person's life. You do not want to miss out on the extraordinary journey this book will lead you on."

— JOE WHITE
President, Kanakuk Kamps

"Adam Barnett has composed a timely and much-needed resource for young people like myself. His message is packed with truth, encouragement, and humor. As you make the transition from high school to college, I highly recommend you read this book. You'll be glad you did!"

— SADIE ROBERTSON
Author, Speaker and Founder of Live Original

"What a MUCH-NEEDED resource! 'Let's Be Honest... Are You Really Ready For College?' is INGENIOUS. I've been in full time youth and young adult ministry for nearly 5 decades now. And repeatedly, as I'm saying my 'farewells' to college students before they leave, my heart often questions if we've 'covered all the bases.' I can't think of a much more appropriate gift for graduating high school seniors than this newly released book. Adam Barnett formatted it brilliantly, as well. I recommend this resource to everyone who works with high school seniors or who has a high school student in their life that they genuinely care about. New books are 'a dime a dozen' these days. But this one is in a league of it's own. Ignore it at your own peril."

— JEANNE MAYO
President, Youth Leader's Coach

What Friends and Colleagues Are Saying

"Adam's passion to see people made whole, his gift of communication and his zeal for the Jesus story is infectious. I pray that through his words you find an abundance of life."

— **Aaron Boyd**
Musician, Writer of *God of This City*
Belfast, Ireland

"'Let's Be Honest' is a must read for every student preparing for college. Adam's practical, challenging and insightful thoughts will help students navigate one of the most crucial transitions of their life. Adam has walked alongside college students for more than a decade. He has faithfully helped them grow in their relationship with Christ in the middle of an increasingly secular culture."

— **Adam Starling**
Senior Pastor, Victory Family Church
Norman, Oklahoma

"This book is a stunning breath of fresh air in its confrontation of the real issues and questions young adults navigate in their college years. This is not only an incredible resource for students heading into their first taste of independence, but it is also a much-needed handbook for parents who have been looking for help to prepare their young adults for the shock and awe of life outside their childhood home. This should be required reading for every high school senior, and for every parent who is intentional about launching their kids from the home with a strong sense of identity and purpose."

— **Amy Little**
Founder, Beautiful Truth Ministries
Norman, Oklahoma

"If ever there were a truly honest book for Christian young people entering college – this is it. For too long the Church has sent its young into a secular minefield, without guidance and without a map. Some survive spiritually. Many do not. Adam Barnett is the real deal and a highly reliable guide. He understands college culture and he knows how it's possible to have a great college experience and a growing friendship with God at the same time. Reading and listening to this book will save a lot of people from unnecessary grief."

— Bill Clark
Senior Pastor, Redeemer Church
Tulsa, Oklahoma

"This is a must read for every high school senior and college freshman. Adam's honest assessment of collegiate life will help students avoid common pitfalls and begin their college experience on the right foot. His insight and candor are refreshing!"

— Brad Baker
Executive Pastor, New Life Church
Colorado Springs, Colorado

"Adam Barnett is a leader of leaders, and through authentic and genuine relationships, he is a charismatic example of Christ's love. His heart to see the Gospel change the future generations creates the light of hope in a dark world."

— Cody Dunbar
Worship Pastor, Council Road Baptist Church; Recording Artist
Oklahoma City, Oklahoma

"As someone who has been around students in both the church and classroom for over a decade, I've grown to appreciate the challenges of addressing effectively these students' needs as they follow Christ. Adam Barnett is someone who has a depth of experience and knowledge that can address these issues in ways that are fruitful. He speaks with grace and truth — a balance that is difficult to maintain, yet essential for speaking into the lives of students."

— Daniel Bunn
Professor of Old Testament, Oral Roberts University
Tulsa, Oklahoma

"Adam Barnett has been an important voice in leading college students through their transition years. This is not a book of theory or ideas. This is a book born out of thousands of real-world relationships with college students. 'Let's Be Honest' turns on the lights, pulls back the curtains, and brings all the toughest issues into the light. For every student and parent who wants to be prepared for the dim, foggy world of college, this book is an invaluable flashlight!"

— Ethan Vanse
Campus Pastor, Church on the Move
Tulsa, Oklahoma

"Adam Barnett is a servant. He is a gifted servant. He loves God and he has a passion for guiding young people. 'Let's be Honest' is simply another way Adam has discovered to help young people grow in their faith while at the same time laughing and crying their way through the process. This book will truly serve any young person if they will merely dive in. It is an easy read but it dives deep into the things that matter. I have no doubt his book will make any person that reads it, young or old, better in some way."

— Jan Ross
Chief of Staff, University of Oklahoma Women's Basketball
Norman, Oklahoma

"Adam and I met when I was an athlete at the University of Oklahoma. I had been looking for someone to talk to about my faith but I was uncomfortable talking about it out loud. Instead of force-feeding me Bible verses, Adam developed a relationship with me that I will always be thankful for. Only after he knew who I truly was did he begin to ask about my faith. As a true friend, Adam not only helped me give my life to Jesus, but he married me to my beautiful wife, Caylee. I will always be thankful to have Adam as a friend and mentor."

— Joe Jon Finley
Football Coach, Texas A & M Football
College Station, Texas

"Adam Barnett has faithfully led thousands of college students and young adults in their faith over the years. He is a passionate, engaging, and authentic orator and author. In a post-modern and globalized world, young people need to be empowered and equipped to not only proclaim the Gospel but live it out as well. Adam has made it his life's work to not only teach others but also model how to live a life worthy of the Gospel. His authentic and uncompromising perspective is like a breath of fresh air."

— Ka'eo Yoshikawa
Youth Pastor, The Well Community Church
Fresno, California

"This book is an extension of the ministry Adam has done for years. Each chapter brings biblical and practical focus to some of the most important and difficult issues students will face. It lays a foundation not only to prepare for college, but will set up the student to thrive and make an impact on people around them. Adam is a man I trust to influence my children. When the time comes, this book will be a must-read for my family."

— Kyle Cantrell
Campus Pastor, Church of the Highlands; Recording Artist
Birmingham, Alabama

"What a timely read. U.S. college dropout rates are tragic. More Americans are going to college than ever before, but only 54 percent of students graduate in six years... six years! Enclosed are clear expectations of what college will look like and how to prepare for it. A must read for students and parents alike."

— Matt Pinnell
Lieutenant Governor, State of Oklahoma
Tulsa, Oklahoma

"Adam has been instrumental in leading college and professional athletes on mission trips to Haiti. I have seen Adam's heart and ministry to college students. He is a strong person of character, a gifted communicator, leader, mentor, husband, and father. He truly has a heart for people, but especially college students."

— Otis Garrison
Vice President, Mission of Hope Haiti
Titanyen, Haiti

"'Let's Be Honest: Are You Really Ready For College?' aims to provide a relevant and Biblical framework for coaching the emerging generation towards a life that thrives through the wonderful challenge of entering college life. This book is perfect for juniors and seniors in high school and is also an excellent resource for youth workers, parents, and pastors helping guide this generation towards a Christ-like life. This book will make a difference and needs to be in the hands of our young people!"

— Tim Ciccone
Director of Youth and Young Adults,
The Evangelical Covenant Church
Chicago, Illinois

"Adam Barnett is one of the best ministry leaders I've ever seen and he is without a doubt an expert in high school and college ministry. His creative, thought provoking, humorous, and intentional leadership have radically impacted thousands of students for years. This is a must have book for parents, students, youth and college ministry leaders, and anyone looking to help students in this pivotal step into young adulthood. Adam hits all the topics that must be faced to approach college with the right heart and mind for Jesus."

— Tim Mannin
Lead Pastor, OKC Community Church
Author of *Doing Things That Matter*
Oklahoma City, Oklahoma

"For the past 15 years, Adam has been investing in students through pastoring and teaching. His heart for students allows him to teach truths authentically and with great transparency. Adam finds creative ways to help young people instruct and navigate this season of life. This book is also for families looking to guide and encourage students during this pivotal time in life."

— Tracy Carlson
Parent and Family Programs Coordinator, University of Oklahoma
Norman, Oklahoma

"Having had the privilege of serving in ministry to college students with Adam for a few years, I can say with confidence that I would recommend this read for any student who is headed off to university. As a pastor, his guidance to anyone in this age range is invaluable. I have yet to encounter anyone better equipped to speak to this season of life in a compelling, truthful, loving-but-sharpening way. I would advise any young soon-to-be-collegiate to read this book, and I would advise any parent of a soon-to-be-collegiate to gift it to their son/daughter; all can trust the fruit herein."

— **Trent Langrehr**
Worship Pastor, City Hope Church; Recording Artist
Mobile, Alabama

"These 90 bite-sized targets, packed with dynamite truths, are what every student needs to digest as they launch to higher education. 'Let's be Honest' lays out the perfect runway to help first year college students land smoothly on campus and avoid a crash. If you want real life wisdom that will lead to a concrete start and finish, this is the tool to get you there!"

— **Ward Wiebe**
Director, K-West Kanakuk Kamps
Branson, Missouri

"Adam Barnett's years of ministry have been consistently marked by one thing: long-term impact. Students that have been under his mentorship continue to ABIDE in Christ long after they are out of high school or college. Adam has never been about a quick fix or flashy advice, but rather sound wisdom and direction that will keep a young person grounded and on a path that leads them into the full life that God has for them. If there is a person in their late teens or early twenties that you care about, you want them to read these words of advice from Adam."

— **Wopsle**
Student Pastor, Redeemer Church
Tulsa, Oklahoma

For my wife and college sweetheart, Andrea...
You are my best friend and a strong woman of God.
Being your husband is the greatest privilege of my life.
I love you, and I love our life together!

For Macy, André, Ellie and Gracía...
Getting to be your Daddy fills my life with joy and
purpose. One day, you'll probably graduate college
and I'll take you off of the family payroll. Until then,
and after then, I'm rooting for you and I love you.

For Dad, Mom, Brandon and Donna...
We don't get to pick our parents, but I still would
have picked you. I am grateful for your constant
encouragement and support. I love you.

For every high school senior, high school graduate, high school
drop out, college freshman, or anyone else about to or hoping to
embark on the expensive and unforgettable journey of college...
I sincerely hope this book helps. May God be with you!

CONTENTS

Part 7: Relationships

Part 8: Spirituality

Part 9: Ten Years From Now

ACKNOWLEDGMENTS

I am a huge fan of Jimmy Fallon. One of the well-known features of The Tonight Show is Jimmy's *Thank You Notes*. He puts pen to paper, cues the *"Thank You Note Song"* by James Poyser, and millions of viewers listen as he comically and sarcastically expresses his gratitude. While millions of people will not read this book (barring a miracle), I started this project with this page. I wanted to write from a place of gratitude. This book would not exist if it were not for a supportive family, enriching relationships, encouraging leaders and inspiring moments throughout my life. Cue the *Thank You Note Song...*

Thank you, **Andrea Barnett**, for marrying me and faithfully putting up with me. Our life together is a great adventure, and being in love, parenting, and ministry with you is such a delight.

Thank you, **Brad Baker**, for being my college pastor. You set the bar high in so many ways. I'm most grateful, though, for the example you gave of loving your bride.

Thank you, **Ward Wiebe**, for being the first spiritual leader in my life to affirm my call to ministry. You awakened something within me. You are my hero.

Thank you, **Rod Conant**, for being the second spiritual leader in my life to affirm my call to ministry. You patiently taught me how to lead a team, write a curriculum, outline a sermon, create a budget, and keep my head down during my swing.

Thank you, **Brooke Harrison**, for being my first boss in vocational ministry. Your leadership started me off on the right foot and you taught me that people always come before projects. You were and still are a wonderful model of leadership.

Thank you, **Joshua and April Thomas, Brandon and Emily Geister, Michael and Amy Wopsle, and Matt and Lisa Pinnell**. You are more than a "small group" — you are family. I enjoy a living room much more when you're in it.

Thank you, **Bill Clark**, for being my pastor, mentor, boss, and friend. You exude the perfect combination of humility, confidence, wisdom, and integrity. I have learned so much from you and I hope to be the leader someday that I see in you.

Thank you, **Redeemer Church staff**, for your invaluable friendship. Serving the Lord next to you is like living a dream. You challenge and inspire me with your love for God and our community. I love praying and playing with you! It is a privilege to experience ministry's best and toughest days next to you.

Thank you, **Redeemer Church**, for being such an incredible family! God's hand is visibly upon our church and it is an honor to worship Him together. You are servant-minded, radically generous, and faithfully committed to prayer. What a joy it is to serve you! Andrea and I love you!

Thank you to our hundreds of ***"Sooners 4 Haiti"*** trip participants, as well as my fearless co-leader and dear friend, **Jan Ross**. I'm grateful for all of the experiences and memories we've made while serving together in Haiti.

Thank you, **Daniel Holdge**, for our invaluable bond. You are my Proverbs 18:24. I appreciate laughing with you, and when you laugh at me.

Thank you, **Joshua Thomas**, for showing me that 1 Samuel 20:17 is possible. Thank you for routing me on, and at times, pushing me along.

Thank you to all of my **former students**. My mind and heart are full of memories with you (retreats, summer camps, small groups, cookouts, worship nights, mission trips, and so on). Sharing in your joy and grief has been my honor. Thank you for trusting me. Leading you has inspired this book. I thank my God every time I remember you (Philippians 1:3).

Thank you to my first college discipleship group — **Riley Cummins, Zac Miller, Brent Potter and Michael Hewett.** You are all now devoted husbands, incredible fathers and faithful ministers of the Gospel. Investing my life into yours was time well spent. I am proud of each of you and your future excites me.

Thank you, **Ryan Broyles, Trey Millard, Ty Darlington, Trevor Knight and Ryan Spangler.** To disciple you taught me so much more about Jesus, the Bible and myself. Thank you for all the difficult questions. I love each of you and am so proud of you.

Thank you, **Tracy Carlson**, for being my partner in crime in college ministry. We saw God move in indescribable ways. I'll never forget how passionately you prayed for our students, and how quickly you showed compassion and grace.

Thank you, **Kristi Tackett** and **Amy Wopsle** for editing this book. What a privilege to have two of my favorite people contribute to this project! I'm grateful for the time you spent to carefully correct my mistakes, like all the unnecessary commas and misspelled wurdz.

Thank you, **Marty Taylor** for your cover design. You are an amazing talent and an even better friend. Thanks for always supporting me in life and ministry. I hope you know how much I appreciate our friendship!

Thank you to my generous **mentors, ministry friends, colleagues and former students** who endorsed this book. Your words mean the world to me! I have great respect for each of you and thank you for your friendship and leadership.

PREFACE

Are You Really Ready for College?

The title of this book is a question I encourage you to honestly answer: *"Are You Really Ready for College?"* I understand the unfairness of asking you this question. After all, you probably haven't started yet. But since you would answer honestly, you certainly land somewhere on the scale between excited and nervous... confident and terrified... enthusiastic and unsure.

When I went to college, I had already watched a variety of movies about the "college experience" that were ridiculous and unrealistic portrayals of what I could expect. There was *Rudy*, which captured the true and inspiring story of a famous college football underdog from the University of Notre Dame. There was *Road Trip*, a vulgar comedy about a college student traveling across the country to save a long distance relationship. There was *Legally Blonde*, where a stereotypical blonde sorority girl is surprisingly accepted into Harvard Law School and shocks her professors and classmates with her success. And who could forget *The Waterboy* with Adam Sandler? After all, it is common for middle-aged men to return to college, only to discover their hidden potential on the football field, right?

Wrong.

Everything you see and hear about the college experience

will not quite compare to *your college experience*. You are unique, and your story is *your story*.

I wrote this book because I have been an eyewitness of countless stories. Thousands. I feel an urgency to share with you what I've seen and learned, and I believe the content of this book will help you make the *most* of your college years, rather than make a *mess* of your college years. On that note, I humbly ask you to trust me! I have seen innumerable college students make the most of their college years, and I have shared in their joy and celebrated their success. Equal in number, I have known those who have made a mess of their college years, and I have been present in their frustration and patiently and lovingly helped them pick up the pieces. That being said, I have some advice to offer. My writing style can be rather blunt at times. I'm not trying to hurt your feelings, but I'm also not concerned if I do. I believe that my honest approach to these pivotal years of your life will help prepare you and guide you along the way.

As you read, you will discover nine parts to this book containing 90 mini-chapters. These are bite-sized sections where I quickly and bluntly share my thoughts on a variety of topics specific to college. As you know, there are approximately three months between your high school graduation and your first day as a freshman in college. You don't necessarily have to read this book during that particular season, but if possible, the 90 days between high school and college is an ideal time to give this book some time and attention.

As you may have already assumed, I write from a Christian perspective. If you are a follower of Jesus, you will relate to some of what I write simply from your experiences in reading the Bible or attending church. If you do not practice the Christian faith, I hope you will still turn the page and keep reading.

Regardless of your personal ideology, my intent in writing this book is not to help get you to heaven, but to help prepare you for college. Then again, Part 8 is about *spirituality*...take it or leave it.

I also write from the perspective of a former college pastor of a very large college ministry. My former students are scattered throughout the nation and world. They are in New York, California, Florida, Haiti, South Africa, Germany, China, and Australia. They are teachers, doctors, dentists, missionaries, and pastors. They are photographers, wedding planners, news anchors, soldiers, and humanitarians. Some are significantly rich and others are living on nickels and dimes. Some are happily married, while others have experienced nasty divorces. Some are parents to multiple children, while others have experienced multiple miscarriages. Some love their jobs and others count the hours until the weekend. Some are meaningfully contributing to their communities while others are drunks or addicts. Some are fervent and passionate in their faith life, while others are still on their journey of discovering God.

I have been a college pastor to thousands of students, and their experiences in college have influenced this book. But I wrote this book for *you* — the individual young man or woman about to embark on an adventurous four-to-seven-year ride called *college*. I pray that God blesses you on your journey, and I thank you for letting me come along.

INTRODUCTION

In my six years as a college pastor, I have vivid memories of one particular day of each year: Freshman Move-In Day. My college ministry staff and I would go to campus wearing matching tank tops with thousands of flyers in our hands to promote our weekly worship night. As time progressed throughout the morning, the parking lot began to slowly fill. Before introducing ourselves to anyone, we'd sit back in the shadows and watch the chaos gradually unfold.

Parents arrived with their overly packed trucks and SUVs. Some had bags strapped to the top of the car, and others even pulled trailers. As they parked and exited their vehicles, we could tell the difference between students who were embarrassed to be seen with their parents, and others who were already anticipating homesickness. At the same time, we saw parents who were reluctant to leave their son or daughter behind, as well as parents who couldn't wait to drive away and were finally empty-nesters *(and excited about it)*.

The month of August is brutally hot in Oklahoma. Many of the dads were also wearing tank tops, showing off their unimpressive, flabby biceps and a thick coat of chest hair. Within 15 minutes, the whole family would be dripping with sweat as they unpacked the bare essentials for the dorm room. The line at the elevator was easily a 20-minute wait, so up the stairs they went. They carried plastic drawers on a cart, laundry baskets, lamps and clothes on hangers. The lucky ones had a microwave. After enduring the heat and getting moved into the dorm room, the students walked their parents back to the car and said goodbye. Some of the exchanges were quick, while others included sincere hugs and tears. Typically, the moms cried until snot ran down their faces. Dads said goodbye to their little girls with a lengthy, tender speech about being careful and making good decisions. Those who had sons offered a firm handshake and a brief speech about becoming a man, *whatever that means*.

Mom and dad drove away. Independence. *Finally*.

I remember meeting students who were overly confident and others who were secretly terrified. Some students couldn't wait for the first day of class. They were busy organizing their class schedule and locating buildings on the campus map so they wouldn't be late for roll call. Some were genuinely interested in grabbing coffee with their roommate to swap stories. They didn't want to live with a total stranger and were intentional to break the ice quickly. Some were looking for details on the party happening that night and couldn't wait to get their hands on a red solo cup. Others were scoping out easy prey, hoping for a casual hookup on their first night on campus. Trust me… I've seen it all. Right there at Freshman Move-In Day, it was easy to see what each individual's priorities were.

I don't know what your situation is back home. Maybe you grew up in safe and healthy home with both of your parents. Maybe you lived with either your father or your mother due to a divorce at some point in your childhood. Maybe a grandparent, aunt and uncle, or older sibling raised you. Maybe you have moved from foster home to foster home, and your dorm or apartment at college will be the most stable home you've ever known. Whoever dropped you off for college has likely given you some sort of advice. Regardless, I'm confident this book will add to your understanding of the years to come and help you prepare.

Not to bore you, but vocational ministry started for me three weeks after I graduated college. I started a 5th-6th-grade ministry at a church in my hometown. Two years later, I served as the junior-high pastor for 7th-8th-grade students. Again, two years later, I became the youth pastor (9th-12th grade students). As you probably assumed, college ministry was next. My experience in ministry is unique. I walked with the same students from the time they were 11-years-old until they received their college degrees. And today, with college ministry in my rearview mirror, I have former students who are married and expecting their second or third child. My investment in student and college ministry has allowed me to witness the greatest joys and challenges associated with *growing up.*

I have also felt the pressure to help students grow up because many of their parents were absent, lazy, naïve, or uninvolved. Some parents were too busy with careers or simply uninterested in spending time with their son or daughter. Others were "present" in the home, but couldn't handle the awkward conversations about, say, *intercourse.* As a youth and college pastor, I had many parents who took a sabbatical from parenting with the expectation that I (and my wife and staff) would fill the void. *But really* — before Andrea and I had our own children, it felt like we were raising a bunch of 18-year-old college students! We've seen and heard it all, which is why I'm happy you have this book in hand. Although we most likely haven't met, I care deeply about you being successful between now and your college graduation.

What does success look like in your college years?

I'm glad you asked. Here are a few possibilities that exist for you:

- Knowing who you are and being proud of who you are
- Maturing from adolescence to adulthood
- Having worthwhile goals and a plan to achieve them
- Maintaining a healthy relationship with your family

- Choosing and contributing to a cause that helps others
- Graduating with a degree and a decent grade point average
- Possessing a healthy work ethic
- Understanding the necessity of wise money management
- Living free from any form of addiction
- Finding love without compromising yourself or another
- Acquiring lifelong friendships and cultivating healthy relationships
- Discovering more about God and the deeper meaning of life

One day, freshman move-in will be a distant memory. You will be wearing a cap and gown at graduation, receiving your college diploma from a faculty member you've probably never met, and you'll be staring your future, dead in the eye. You'll be packing your apartment, saying goodbye to your roommates, and moving away to start your career. Depending on your grades and interview skills, you may be moving back home into your parent's basement.

Whatever your future looks like, I'm confident this book can help point you in a positive and healthy direction. And for crying out loud, don't just skip to part five because you want to read about sex. Read it all.

Oh, and if you read this before moving away to college, make sure you walk your parents (or whoever cared enough to drop you off) to the car and give them a genuine, long hug. Don't rush this moment. Tell them, as best as you know how, that you are grateful for all they've done to help you get to this day. That moment will be good practice to stop and show respect and gratitude for anyone who helps you along your journey. God knows, you're going to need all the help you can get.

Now, let the preparation begin.

PART ONE
WHO ARE YOU?

Sounds like a pretty dumb question, doesn't it? But, *really.* Who are you? You could obviously answer that question with a variety of totally rational descriptions. Who you are, to some degree, can be related to your parents, your family of origin and where you were born. For example, my children are forced to be fans of the University of Oklahoma football team solely because my wife and I graduated from OU. To cheer for any other University would be considered the highest level of treason. It's in our family's blood.

Who you are can also be defined by your passions and your ambitions. As you meet new people throughout college, one of the first questions they will ask you is, *"What are you studying?"* To some, the question, *"Who are you?"* can casually be answered, *"I'm a communications major."* (By the way, this doesn't change once you enter your career. Within a few minutes of meeting someone new, they want to know, *"What do you do?"* This quickly allows them to assume your annual salary, which quickly spirals into a nasty series of comparisons.) It is wise to learn now: what you do doesn't define who you are.

This question reaches deep into your core. It reaches further than where you're from, what your family is like, what your passions and interests are, and what you decide to study in college. I invite you to zoom out of the obvious and take a more holistic snapshot of the person you are. Many college students will procrastinate answering this question. The tendency is to focus on the "college experience," working just enough to score decent grades (C's for degrees, right?), sleeping in, socializing and taking it easy. Many college students graduate and look back on their college years only to discover an embarrassing amount of wasted time. By the way, that is time you cannot get back. Ever.

Clinical psychologist and author Meg Jay says that the ages 20-29 are a *"pivotal time when the things we do — and the things we don't do — will have an enormous effect across years and even generations to come.*"[1] I completely agree, but I believe her statement very much applies to the college experience too. In the words of social commentator Kay Hymowitz, *"Adults don't emerge. They're made."* You are not too young to begin answering these questions. What is making you? What is shaping you? Who are the people and what are the experiences that are responsible for the greatest impact on your life?

Who are you?

CHAPTER 1

Two Tough Questions

"Maybe we are supposed to think and dream much more about who we are becoming instead of what we are doing." — Tim Mannin

Tim Mannin is a friend that I intentionally keep close. He asks tough questions. He is a man of few words, but when he gets going, what he has to say is profoundly helpful. Over a decade ago, I heard him ask two questions that have stuck in my mind all these years. Actually, these questions occasionally bother me (in a good way). To coast through life without intentional moments of self-reflection is to rob yourself of discovering and reaching your potential. The following two questions are ones that invite serious self-evaluation. They are questions that *hold you accountable* to *hold yourself accountable*. I'd like to ask you these questions now, and I dare you to muster up an honest answer:

1. Who are you becoming?
2. Do you like who you are becoming?

The first question invites a reflection on the present and

what you hope for in the future. What are your physical and psychological characteristics? How does your family of origin operate? How healthy are your relationships? What are your life experiences and how do they shape your thinking? Author Klyne Snodgrass says, *"We have difficulties, successes, traumas, embarrassments, and knowledge-enhancing experiences. All these things shape our identity; they make us who we are."*[2] So what are your difficulties, successes, traumas, embarrassments, and knowledge-enhancing experiences? Stop and think about it. How are they influencing who you are becoming?

Who and what are you faithful to? What cuts deeper to the core of your allegiance than a national flag or university sports team ever could? What are you intensely committed to? What are your dreams? I encourage you to grab a piece of paper and a pen and seriously answer these questions.

If you have a hard time answering these questions, don't be discouraged. The past has a significant influence on who you are today, but it doesn't have the final word on tomorrow. Tomorrow is unwritten. It is untouched and undetermined. No matter what the past holds, tomorrow is saturated with potential and opportunity. In trying to answer, *"who are you becoming,"* today is a great time to think about the possibilities that exist in tomorrow! In his book, *Doing Things that Matter,* Mannin offers a great insight that applies to your college years: *"Pursuing the question of 'who am I becoming' is a journey."*[3] I couldn't agree more, so buckle up.

The second question is one that invites a more sobering reflection. You certainly have an idea of who you are becoming. But, do you like that person? Are you proud of that person? As you fast-forward in your mind, what do you see in ten years? Twenty years? It is possible that your answer is, "I absolutely *do not like* who I am becoming." If so, take a deep breath and chill out for a moment. The purpose in asking you this question is to motivate an honest scan of your life, and to see how you feel about what you see. As you examine your life, consider:

- What is my identity rooted in?
- Are my relationships healthy?
- What are my goals and ambitions?
- Are my motivations pure?
- What kind of life am I living when no one is watching?

If you don't like what you see, there is time to choose a different course and pursue an extraordinary future. But the time to do so is *now*. Not after you graduate college. Not after you find your spouse. Not after you land a job or have children or become financially secure. Today is the day. And remember: never place your identity in anything that can be taken away from you, such as a relationship, a degree, a job, or a salary. All of those things can vanish in a split second, so build *who you are* and *who you are becoming* around something that will last.

CHAPTER 2

Voices Around You

"Don't let someone else's opinion of you become your reality." — Les Brown

Our youngest daughter, Macy, is our most unpredictable and rambunctious child. She is the life of the party and wears her emotions on her sleeve. She is also very tenderhearted and takes words personally. Sticks and stones could break her bones, and words really hurt her, too. Actually, they devastate her.

In Kindergarten, Macy took an impressive fall and hit her front tooth on the concrete. Luckily, it didn't knock the tooth out or cause any long-term damage. The root soon died, leaving the outside of the tooth an unappealing shade of brown. While playing outside in the neighborhood one evening, a boy called Macy "brown tooth." She ran home screaming and crying and her spirit was crushed. My son, Andre, discovered what happened and slugged the boy who insulted his little sister.

Although I gave Andre the *"we don't punch people"* speech, I must admit, I was a little proud. No one messes with our baby Macy and gets away with it!

"Brown tooth" haunted Macy for months, and I actually think she prayed to the Tooth Fairy that her brown tooth would fall out. Credit the tooth fairy, or God, or gravity, but the tooth finally fell out. Macy delicately placed it under her pillow, and the next morning, she screamed with joy — she awakened to a ten-dollar bill. Not a bad price tag on a tooth, but not enough to buy back the emotional pain caused by one comment from a boy down the street.

Brown tooth. Fat. Skinny. Superficial. Rude. Easy. Virgin. Religious. Nerd. Jock. Weird. Stupid. Different. Loser. Strange. Spoiled. Stuck up. Poor. Ugly. The list goes on and on. And just to be clear, the pain from hurtful titles only intensifies from kindergarten to college. "Brown tooth" might feel like a compliment compared to some of the insults we all hear throughout our lives.

For you, the opposite may be true. You may come from an incredibly supportive, loving, affirming home. Your parents may have attended every event you ever participated in and awarded you cash for good grades. You've been called beautiful and talented and smart and pretty much perfect your entire life. Your confidence may be built on years of compliments offered from your parents, teachers, coaches, and friends.

No doubt about it, you have voices that speak into your life and your identity. These voices have been positive or negative, or a blend of the two. Some of the voices have hurt you and some of the voices have helped you. Regardless, *these voices don't define you.* Don't allow what others say about you have the slightest impact on your self-worth. Their voices don't mean diddly-squat compared to what God says about you.

I'm aware that your beliefs and mine may not fully align. That's ok. Just keep reading. I will address spirituality in Part Eight of this book, but there is a lot to read between here and there.

CHAPTER 3

Chameleon People

"Be yourself. Everyone else is already taken." — Oscar Wilde

Chameleons are lizards that specialize in changing color. They adapt to their environment as a safety mechanism, making it much less likely to be noticed by a predator. As people, we can act like chameleons. Whatever social setting we find ourselves in, we can blend in like everyone else around us. We do this as a safety mechanism, making our differences less noticeable.

Don't be a chameleon.

It is safe to say, there is not one single human in the world that has your exact personality (I can't scientifically prove that statement is true, nor do I have time to try, but I stand by it). You are uniquely wired. You are special. You are one of a kind! But I'm warning you — in your college years, you will feel the pressure to abandon your personality to blend in with everyone else. Chameleon people have different personalities around friends, church friends, roommates, and family. And when those people find out that you act one way here and another way there, you're looking at an explosion of drama and a splitting headache.

Don't allow anyone to force you to change in order to fit in or belong. To do so is to compromise one of God's greatest gifts to you — your personality. Be you. Be consistently you.

CHAPTER 4

Your Purpose

"Purpose is the place where your deep gladness meets the world's needs." — Frederick Buechner

Certainly discovering your purpose has crossed your mind at some point already. Rick Warren wrote *The Purpose Driven Life*, a book that has been on the New York Times Best Seller list for one of the longest periods in history (the dude sold 30 million copies in the first five years after it was released). On the cover reads an intimidating question: *"What on Earth am I here for?"* Pretty good question, huh?

You only have one life to live. What are you going to do with it? Is your priority to make your family proud? To find a secure and well-paying career? To maintain a good reputation and close friendships? To meet your mate, fall in love and be married happily ever after, inevitably resulting in 2.5 children, a golden retriever, and a white picket fence?

I think we all want to make a difference in the world. In our childhood, we run around the house with bed sheets as capes, boldly declaring to onlookers that we have come to save the day. The fate of the whole world was in our hands, and we had full confidence in our ability to save the human race. And then we grew up. We realize how big the world is, how enormous its problems are, and how small and insignificant one individual is. We stop dreaming and our ambitions shrink. We become self-absorbed and only dream about that boring, white picket fence.

When I was little, I watched a show called *MacGyver*. It aired from 1985 to 1992, and the main character was my hero. In every single episode, he was expected to save the world (I did some research here, but in 8 seasons, MacGyver saved the world 139 times!). As a little boy, I fantasized about situations like MacGyver's in which I would save the world and be saluted as a hero to all of humanity. But today, I think the idea of heroism is much different. It doesn't include missiles and parachutes (not for me, at least). It includes waking up every morning with a clear understanding of my purpose, and squeezing each day like a sponge to get every bit that the day may offer.

When I was in college, I read the following statement from author John Piper, and it continues to motivate me today:

> *"You don't have to know a lot of things for your life to make a lasting difference in the world. But you do have to know the few great things that matter, and then be willing to live for them and die for them. The people that make a durable difference in the world are not the people who have mastered many things, but who have been mastered by a few great things. If you want your life to count, if you want the ripple effect of the pebbles you drop to become waves that reach the ends of the earth and roll on for centuries and into eternity, you don't have to have a high IQ; you don't have to have good looks or riches; you don't have to come from a fine family or a fine school. You have to know a few, great, majestic, unchanging, obvious, simple, glorious things, and be set on fire by them."*[4]

I assure you, no matter what you achieve and acquire in this life, especially within the North American context of wealth, prosperity and opportunity, you will never be content. You'll always want more. But if what you seek in this life is beyond achievements and acquisitions, if what you seek is discovering and flourishing within your purpose, you will discover a deep sense of fulfillment. Ultimately, in the words of my friend, Tim: *"God has created us for more than what most of us are living. Too many of us have been pulled into a normal life. As a result, we find ourselves chasing the American standard of normal instead of reimagining what's possible. Be wary of becoming a casualty of normalcy."*[5]

Let that thought linger for a moment, and be sure to see the connection between normalcy and casualty. I realize your near future might include general calculus or statistics, but I've made up an equation that I hope you'll remember:

Comfort + Normalcy − (Passion x Purpose) = Casualty.

If your purpose is lost in trivial *(unimportant, insignificant, petty, frivolous, marginal, irrelevant)* things, you suffer with normalcy. Don't be another victim of the mundane American Dream. For crying out loud, find your purpose, and chase it!

CHAPTER 5

Your Thoughts

*"Life is a reflection of what you think. If
your thoughts are negative, the world you
see will be the same."* — Leon Brown

My family knows that I love to impress people with my medical knowledge. I can rattle off all sorts of insights on the functions of the endoplasmic reticulum, ribosomal cavity and mitochondrion, and the critical role they play in our survival. But, I'm a fraud. I barely passed Anatomy class in college. Still, this kind of stuff interests me. So let's talk about your brain.

Has this thought ever occurred to you: *what happens when a thought occurs to you?* To complicate this, right now you are having thoughts about whether or not you've thought about what happens when thoughts occur to you. Have a headache?

Your brain is composed of about 100 billion nerve cells (neurons) interconnected by trillions of synapses. On average, each connection transmits about one signal per second. Somehow, that's producing a thought. As you're reading this, there is an electrical signal between 100 billion nerve cells, and as the signal reaches the end of an axon, it causes the release of a chemical neurotransmitter into the synapses. A target neuron responds with its own electrical signal, which then spreads to other neurons. Within a few hundred milliseconds, the signal spreads to billions of neurons in interconnected areas of the brain. As a result of everything you just read, you just had a thought...and you didn't even break a sweat. If you check the facts on my medical rambling, you might find an error. I'm not an expert... I'm simply attempting to prove the point that your brain is an extraordinarily powerful organ, and life seems smoother when you use it. The *thought* about how *thoughts* occur to us is a pretty remarkable *thought*, don't you *think*?

Unfortunately, this remarkable thing called a "thought" is under constant attack from an enemy called "negativity." I'm not telling you to live your life as a raging optimist that never has a bad day. My wife is incredibly optimistic. Like, I'm talking way too happy all the time. Sometimes, she's so happy that I just think she lacks information (I'm admitting that I'm a realist). But being a pessimist is really no healthy way to live. Shake those negative thoughts off and win the war that takes place daily in the battleground of your mind!

Part of winning this war is resisting and refusing a nasty four-letter word that people may speak over your life. The nasty four-letter word is: *can't.* You can't. You simply can't. You can't make the grades. You can't graduate. You can't be sober. You can't find a mate. You can't please your parents. You can't succeed. People who regularly apply the word "can't" to life are not worth listening to. I like how Henry Ford said it: *"Whether you believe you can do a think or not, you are right."*[6]

As you attempt to maintain healthy, positive thoughts, remember that a battlefield is unpredictable. Sometimes you advance, while other times you run for your life. Our thoughts may lead us forward one day and backward the next. Do your best to commit to positivity and refuse to listen to those who pull you down with negativity. Much of your well-being, both during college and for the rest of your life, is your ability to use your brain in a productive, positive manner.

CHAPTER 6

Set Goals

*"A goal should scare you a little and
excite you a lot."* — Joe Vitale

Goals are important, and the loftier, the better. But still, they should be realistic. Norman Vincent Peale is famous for his well-intentioned motivational quote: *"Shoot for the moon, and if you miss, you'll land among the stars."* I get the point — if you're aiming at something great, even if you don't achieve it, you'll still be somewhere better than where you started. While this is motivating, I'm not fully buying it.

Let's get technical. If you shoot for the moon, your goal is 238,855 miles from the earth. If you miss, you're not among the stars. The nearest star (other than the sun) is 25 trillion miles away. Trillion. So actually, if you shoot for the moon and miss, you'll be floating in the dead cold of space where you can't breathe, where your eyes would explode, and where no one can hear you scream. Not good. So I say shoot for the moon, and if you miss, reload and shoot again.

Oh, and your goals need to be *realistic*.

Graduating with a degree in Mechanical Engineering in two years — probably not realistic. Landing a seven-digit paycheck (plus benefits) in the first year of your career — unlikely. Putting a ring on her finger after one date — doubt it. Realistic goals are not like New Year's resolutions. Every January, the gym is packed with people who want to lose 40 pounds in 30 days, and when February arrives, the gym is a ghost town. Come on. Placing unrealistically high expectations on yourself will result in higher disappointments.

Early in my vocational ministry, I learned an acronym that holds me accountable to setting realistic goals. It takes the pressure off of improbable time frames and unlikely results. I hope this will help you, too. Set "SMART" Goals:

S: Specific
M: Measurable
A: Attainable
R: Relevant
T: Time Based

Filter all of your goals through these criteria and you're aimed at the bullseye of success. Ok, actually, if you've ever thrown darts, hitting the middle circle is hard. According to my math, $[1(1-0.2)=0.81(1-0.2)=0.8][(0.8)^5=0.327]$, you have a 0.02% chance of hitting the bullseye on any one shot.[7] So even setting SMART Goals doesn't guarantee success every time. So, when you shoot for the moon or aim at the bullseye and miss, well, read the next chapter.

CHAPTER 7

Learn From Failure

"I've missed more than 9,000 shots in my career. I've lost almost 300 games. 26 times, I've been trusted to take the game winning shot and missed. I've failed over and over and over again in my life, and that is why I succeed." — Michael Jordan

I'm a huge Michael Jordan fan. As a matter of fact, I'm appalled every time I hear someone make the pathetic argument that Kobe Bryant or LeBron James are as good as or better than MJ *(if you think I'm wrong, come at me)*. People that make that argument either lack intelligence or just don't understand basketball. As a child, I religiously sat with my old man in his blue La-Z-Boy recliner and watched the Chicago Bulls play on TNT. It was shocking any time we watched them lose. They were *amazing*. But they had flaws. They had bad games. They lacked chemistry every once in a while. And some nights, an opponent simply couldn't miss and couldn't be stopped. Even the best in the business experience defeat. In case you need supportive evidence:

- Abraham Lincoln was defeated in a race to become a United States Senator. He went on to become one of the most decorated, successful presidents in the history of the United States.

- Albert Einstein failed to pass the exam to enter a tech school located in Zurich, Switzerland. Only 26 years later, he was known for his Theory of Relativity and the beginnings of Quantum Theory, and for winning the 1921 Nobel Prize.

- Bill Gates' first company was a complete disaster. Today, he is worth nearly $100B and is contributing world-changing humanitarian relief to poverty-ridden nations.

- Theodor Seuss Geisel's (Dr. Seuss) first manuscript was rejected 28 times. By the time of his death, he had sold over 600 million copies of his books, which have been translated into 20 different languages.

- Elvis Presley walked his first demo disc into Sun Records, was turned away and told, "You can't sing." Persistently sticking to his dream, his records have sold over 1 billion copies worldwide.

- Katy Perry's first album only sold 200 copies. Enough said.

- Oprah Winfrey had a difficult childhood, raised in poverty by a single teenage mother and her grandmother. After various setbacks in her childhood, she had a chance to co-anchor the news, but was removed for being "unfit for television." Today, she is a multi-billionaire and internationally famous.

- Walt Disney was a writer for a local newspaper, but was fired by the editor for lacking imagination. He started his own company, Laugh-O-Gram, producing cartoon animations. While he saw some success, he was eventually required to file for bankruptcy. Years later, as you know, Disney found success, as his movies are all you watched in your childhood.[8]

I'm hopeful that you get the point. Words used to describe the stories above include: *defeated, failed, disaster, rejected, turned away, released, fired, setback,* and *removed.* But each story also represents people who took responsibility when something didn't go as planned and didn't make excuses. They didn't point fingers or cast blame on others. They just pulled up their bootstraps. They embody the old William Hickson proverb:

This is a lesson you should heed:

Try, try, try again.

If at first you don't succeed,

Try, try, try again.[9]

Each of us will face moments when something doesn't work out the way we hoped. You might fail a class. You might fail a friend. You might fail at a job. You might fail morally. You might fail in reaching your goals. I hate to tell you, you *will probably fail at something.* But if you never fail at anything, you might not be trying hard enough in general. Yes, failure is disappointing and discouraging. But take it on the chin. Then, keep your chin up. Move forward. As 6-time NBA Champion Michael Jordan so eloquently put it, "I can accept failure. Everyone fails at something. What I cannot accept is not trying."

So *when* you fail, keep going and try again. Make an effort, not an excuse. Or as my father-in-law says, "Always be up, or getting up."

CHAPTER 8

Find Your Passions

*"Chase down your passion like it's the last
bus of the night."* — Terri Guillemets

In between our junior and senior years in college, Andrea and I spent a good part of the summer in India. We had been married for less than a year when we embarked on one of the most difficult trips of our lives. In New Delhi, the temperatures reached an overwhelming 115° F. I've never seen my urine darker than it was that summer.

Midway through our trip, we flew to Ladakh, India, where we trekked through the Himalayan Mountains, drank Yak Butter Tea, served in a Buddhist village, and cooked homemade chicken noodle soup over a campfire at night (by the way, don't ever let your wife name chickens when your intent all along is to kill and eat them). The temperatures at night were well below freezing, so we sure loved the feeling of the morning sun on our faces. We scrambled eggs and boiled coffee over the fire and packed up our tents. After extinguishing the embers in the fire *(with the dark gold urine previously mentioned)*, our trek would continue. Within half an hour, at least one of us had to yield to the poop-inducing power of coffee and find a place to squat. When you got to go, you got to go. Even the extreme temperatures didn't matter. Fun memories in our first year of marriage, huh?

This somewhat ridiculous experience in India gave Andrea and me more than an archive of both miserable and mesmerizing memories. It lit a passion within us. A passion for the world and a passion for the orphan. In India, we were surrounded by homeless children on the streets. They wore weathered potato sacks and they were dirty, skinny, and hopeless. I'll never forget one boy that begged us for food. I could literally see hundreds of bugs crawling through his hair, which probably hadn't been cut or shampooed in years. I can't begin to tell you how much my heart broke. My wife's heart was shattered into pieces, too.

There's a song by Brooke Frasier in which she sings the following lyrics: *"Now that I have seen, I am responsible."* This is a very accurate summary of the way Andrea and I felt surrounded by a sea of helpless children. Could we help all of them? No. But right there in a dirty train station in Chandigarh, India, two overwhelmed, madly in love 21-year-olds shook hands with one another and God: *we will do our part to help,* we prayed. We didn't know how many biological children we would have, if any. We didn't know how much it would cost, or from where, or how many, or how old, or what gender. What we did know — we were sharing a moment that would change our lives forever. We felt passion for the orphan, and we decided to do our part. We agreed that one day we would adopt.

Fast forward: my wife delivered our first daughter, Ellie, in 2009 and our second daughter, Macy, in 2012. Life was perfect. We were a cute little family of four that could fit in a normal sized car and eat fast food for under twenty dollars. We had some money in the bank and plenty of leisure time to share as a family. Amazing wife. Check. Two adorable girls. Check. A dog. Check. A white, picket fence. Nope. We didn't have one of those, but I was living my American Dream, and I loved it.

For a few years, I felt super comfortable living my American Dream, but then my heart started feeling discontent. When you're passionate about something, it'll pester you until you pursue it. A promise is a promise. The passion for the orphan that had been planted in the soil of our hearts years earlier was starting to sprout. Do you know how scary it is to learn the price of international adoption and then realize it costs more than what you have in your savings account? Absolutely terrifying! My memory of the brown-eyed boy with bugs in his hair wouldn't leave me alone. While I had no clue if that boy was even still alive, I was determined to help another orphan survive. So, we began the long paperwork pregnancy of international adoption.

As you know, some couples go to the doctor for an ultrasound and hear these life-altering and budget-altering words: "you're pregnant, with twins." Some respond with "oh, wonderful, praise the Lord!" Others stare into space as if their entire life was just stripped away from them in one gut-punching announcement. One evening, our adoption agency contacted my wife with life-altering news. She shared it with me that night over dinner.

"They have a little boy in the Democratic Republic of Congo. His mother and father are both dead and his health is failing." My heart jumped for joy and the time to take action had arrived. I was swelling with excitement and started envisioning all the joys of having a son. Finally... I'd have someone to watch football with me! And then, Andrea continued.

"And he has an older sister. She's eight or nine years old."

Long, awkward silence.

"I'm sorry, what did you just say?"

"What... did... you... just... say?"

Because of the passion deposited in our hearts as wide-eyed 21-year-old kids in India, our reaction quickly evolved from "what did you just say?" to "what are we waiting for?" These kids needed us. They needed *someone!* In 2013, we accepted our agency's match and agreed to become mommy and daddy to Gracía Marie Otakombe and André Eseme.

I had been to the Democratic Republic of Congo before in 2009. Upon returning home, I remember telling my wife, "I never want to go back to that place." So when we were matched with children there, I couldn't decide between laughing and crying. As I'm writing this book, the DRC is expected to be the poorest country in the world for the next four years. It is a really difficult place to survive, especially for homeless, defenseless orphans. What better place to rescue children from despair than the most desperate country on the planet?

It was time to go. Bags were packed. Ellie and Macy were oozing with excitement. Dear friends filled our home the night before we left and covered us in prayer. Off we went. On October 6th, 2015, we boarded a plane and headed to the DRC. Upon arrival, we quickly discovered that Andre didn't look well. Malaria had taken a toll on his little body (He was 5-years-old and weighed less than 30 pounds). We quickly found a doctor and hooked him up to IVs and started him on medication. Over the next ten days, we continued Andre's medication, diligently completed all of our necessary paperwork, bonded with our two new children, and survived an attempted robbery in which three men fired pistols at the house we were staying in. Seriously, for a moment we thought: *"there's no chance we're getting out of here."*

On October 13th, 2015, we were ready to leave. But, as expected in many African nations, the government did not issue us exit letters. Our children were *stuck*. They weren't allowed to leave the country, and they certainly weren't going to walk through an airport without exit letters. Our plane tickets home were trashed, as we couldn't leave from the DRC. So, we prayed in faith and booked four tickets home from a neighboring country. We made it home on October 15th, 2015. Safe.

If we never went to India *(as college students)*, I'm not sure we would have adopted. Maybe our eyes would have never opened to the orphan crisis in the first place. Maybe our hearts would have never broken. I'm so thankful for India. I'm thankful that I got to cross paths with the brown-eyed boy in the potato sack, because when I looked in his eyes, something changed in me forever. Something that we experienced in college prompted us to adopt two children ten years later!

Your college years are a great time to begin finding a cause that you are passionate about. Discover something that will keep you up at night. Something that will require radical commitment and resiliency. Something that others may judge as stupid or ridiculous or crazy or risky. Where do your deep gladness and the needs of the world meet? Where are you ready to give your time and energy and influence and money and prayer?

If you have no stinking clue what you're passionate about, let me offer a list of examples. Certainly, this is not an exhaustive list, but hopefully this can get the wheels in your mind turning.

- Honoring our troops with care packages
- Caring for the families of fallen soldiers
- Assisting the disabled
- Serving single mothers
- Aiding the widow
- Advocating for the orphan

- Raising awareness of social injustices
- Contributing to the local church
- Supporting the movement to end sex slavery
- Participating in local or international projects
- Joining teams bringing relief after natural disasters
- Visiting children in the hospital with balloons
- Using your voice to prevent abuse and bullying
- Tutoring young kids in your local school system
- Assisting in your local animal shelter
- Providing meals and blankets for the homeless

The list goes on and on. World peace. Disease control. Wildlife protection. Forest preservation. World hunger. Clean drinking water. Mental health. Women's rights. Environmental issues. Blood donation. Drunk driving awareness. Racial reconciliation. Literacy. Prevention of suicide, rape, poverty, violence, crime, corruption, malaria or child labor.

You have time and talent and influence and resources.

Use your voice.

Take a stand.

Raise some money.

Here me loud and clear: the world needs you. Good luck finding your passion or your cause, because when you do, the world will never be the same.

CHAPTER 9

You Have a Choice

"No matter what your situation is, remind yourself: 'I have a choice.'" — Deepak Chopra

I'm not sure who the first parent was to ever ask this question, but it is brilliant: "if your friends jumped off of a bridge, would you?" I'm sure you've heard that question before. The obvious implication: just because someone else is doing it, you don't have to also. As you navigate the waters of independence, you'll quickly notice that swimming is much easier when you make the right choices. Right choices are ones that reflect your personal values, rather than what will massage your fragile ego or make another person happy.

As a college pastor, I had students who dated the wrong person because they didn't want to be single. Others pursued a degree that their parents had chosen for them. Some got sloppy drunk just to fit in with the crowd or had sex with complete strangers simply because they enjoyed the feeling of being wanted. I had students who carelessly used their parent's credit cards, hit snooze and missed class, and chose to drive after one too many drinks.

You aren't exempt from making poor choices. We all say things we shouldn't, buy things we can't afford, hurt people we love, and do things we regret. Hopefully your poor choices are infrequent and you have enough humility to admit your stupidity when you make a mistake. Oh, but don't just admit you messed up. Learn from it, and don't make the same choice again!

Here are three suggestions related to your decision making in college:

1. Compromise is a dirty little thief. If a choice you make compromises your character, your dreams, your honesty, your purity or your word, you've officially been robbed. Whatever you do, don't make a choice that doesn't represent who you are because of a peer-pressure from friends. It's time to grow up. Peer-pressure is something we all dealt with starting in elementary school. Remember when your classmate dared you to eat glue and you did it? That was a decade ago. You're old and mature enough now to know your values and to not compromise those values in order to please your buddies or strangers. Tell them to get lost and you'll sleep much more peacefully in the end.

2. When you make a compromise, don't make an excuse. Make an effort to resolve the situation and take responsibility. If you get in the habit of making excuses as a college student, you'll attempt to continue the pattern in adulthood. Excuses don't work with your spouse, your children, your boss, or your bank. Taking responsibility means resisting the urge to point fingers and cast blame elsewhere, and also guarantees a higher possibility that others will show grace and understanding. When you dump all of your excuses, you are more likely to learn and grow from your mistakes.

3. Poor choices deliver consequences. Own them. Consequences are very challenging to accept, but how you handle difficulties and challenges in your life greatly influences the kind of person you're becoming. When you were little, consequences may have included a confession, an apology, a spanking, or time out. This isn't rocket science: unprotected sex, cheating on an exam, lying to your parent, skipping class, or driving under the influence will leave you wishing you could rewind to your childhood and be put in time out. Life is already hard, but the more poor choices you make, life may begin to feel rather cruel. So here I am — waving the flag and sounding the alarm: if you make a poor choice, don't be surprised if consequences come knocking on your door. You've earned them.

CHAPTER 10

Your Insecurities

*"I have insecurities, of course, but
I don't hang out with anyone who
points them out to me."* — Adele

Stage of Life is a storytelling site that did research on high
school students and their idea of self-worth. The results
of their research are sickening. In a national poll, ninety-five
percent (95%) of teenagers have felt inferior at some point in
their lives. The teens were asked to identify their top insecurities
that relate to their self-worth. In order, the answers were:
appearance, ability, intelligence, size, age, race, gender, family
economic status, religion and sexual orientation.[10] It is natural
to think about what others think about you, but something is
more stomach-turning from this research.

Forty-one percent (41%) of teenagers have purposely tried to
make another person feel inferior. Clearly, some teens admitted
to dissing a classmate because he or she simply doesn't like the
person. One third of those teens are disrespectful to others
because they like to feel powerful. But half of the teens who
admitted to being rude for no reason give a disheartening
reason: they point out other people's flaws to feel better about
their own flaws. Essentially, low self-esteem can spread faster
than the flu in your dorms.

Just so you know, you have insecurities. You can disagree with me all day long, but trust me, I'm right. To have insecurities is to be human, but to let your insecurities define you and cripple you is to be a victim. So fight them. Fight them aggressively so that you are occasionally pestered by your insecurities rather than constantly destroyed by them. One of the most important steps in fighting your insecurities is admitting them, so take some time to ponder what yours may be. Then, put them in their place. And for crying out loud, don't let your insecurities lead you to tear others down so you feel better about yourself.

CHAPTER 11

Born into Privilege

"And with privilege goes responsibility."
— John F. Kennedy

If you are reading this as a citizen of the United States of America (or any other nation of privilege), it will serve you and the world well if you acknowledge what has been given to you and use it wisely and responsibly. The USA is called the "land of opportunity" for a reason. The opportunities are endless. Privilege comes in a variety of forms: the color of your skin, the money in your account, the opportunity for education, and the support from a family. To be frank, the more naïve you are about your privileges, the more you will unknowingly hurt people and be viewed as entitled and self-centered. Instead, approach your privileges with humility and leverage those privileges to create positive change in the world.

I have traveled to Haiti twenty times and the place feels like a home away from home. The first time our children traveled to Haiti with us, I witnessed their sobering reaction to privilege. We were with the poorest of poor in remote villages where children wear no clothes, adults have no jobs, and food and water are not guaranteed. We shared unforgettable moments of prayer and laughter with the Haitian people in their very small homes (what our culture would refer to as "shacks"), and our children weren't united by money or position or nationality, but instead, a soccer ball and the hot Caribbean sun. During our evenings together, our children revealed their "culture shock" from their experiences during the day. They asked, *"Why didn't the children today have clothes? Why were they barefoot? They were hungry. Why, daddy? Why?"* Good questions, kiddos. Umm, the answer is convicting and easy: it all comes down to where they were born.

Mostly on foreign soil, I've felt a heightened awareness of my privilege. Certain moments have dropped me to my knees with compassion and caused me to weep. In Rwanda, I met people whose spouses and children were brutally murdered with machetes in the 1994 genocide. In India, I met individuals whose lives were threatened because of their faith. In Egypt, I met an Iraqi refugee whose 14-year-old son was dragged from their home and killed by Islamic terrorists. In Mozambique, I walked through miles of trash that thousands of people call home. In the Philippines, I was followed by thieves who eventually stole my passport and all of my money. In South Africa, I was bribed while trying to exit the country. From the Democratic Republic of Congo, my wife and I adopted two children who were sick, hungry and homeless. My friends, let's be real. If you wake up and go about your day without dealing with genocide, persecution, war, poverty, crime, corruption, or hunger, *you are privileged.*

For further perspective, here are a few realities that you should allow to sink in. Should you read through these quickly without feeling an ounce of compassion and/or gratitude, you might be naïve about how fortunate you really are. But if you read these and they punch you in the gut, you are on your way to understanding the reality of privilege. Maybe these are privileges you've never thought about before:

- You have clean drinking water. Millions of people around the world walk hours each day to obtain water, and often carry full water jugs back to their homes or villages. Consider this: every 90 seconds, a child dies due to water related illnesses. Close to one billion people live without access to clean drinking water.[11]

- You have Imodium and ibuprofen. Diarrhea and fever kills millions of people each year. Throughout your childhood, you've pooped your pants and had a temperature countless times, but mommy always had a bottle of preventative medications in the cabinet.

- You got a basic education: kindergarten to high school. In most countries, school is not prioritized, expected, or possible. Instead of reading, writing and arithmetic, children around the world focus their morning on fetching a bucket of unsanitary drinking water for the family.

- You are safe. Every day, thousands of faithful men and women are thinking about your protection and they are willing to give their lives in order to defend you from harm. They are the Air Force, Army, Coast Guard, Marines, and Navy. While you are worried about turning in your research paper on time, young people around the world are thinking about threats from ISIS, the Taliban, Al-Qaeda, and the LRA.

- You are free. You can vote. You can speak up. You can worship. You will not be arrested for posting a political opinion on Facebook. You are not forced by the government to worship a particular god. The freedom of choice is not common around the world.

- You have access to whatever you need. In many places of the world, if a water pump or tire axle breaks, you either go without or have to wait 6-9 months to afford a replacement. You can walk into Wal-Mart or Target or order from Amazon Prime and get whatever you need in a matter of minutes or two-day delivery. Your access to medication and food isn't subjected to economic or political corruption. You simply drive to CVS or Whole Foods and get what you need.

- You have reliable infrastructure. Street lights illuminate neighborhoods and highways. Electricity is available 24/7/365. I'll never forget driving down the highway outside of Monrovia, Liberia, when a streetlight came on. The driver stopped in the middle of the road and emotionally shared, "I haven't seen a streetlight on here in over ten years."

- You can dream big. You can start a band in your garage and ten years later, you might sell 100,000 albums on iTunes. You can start your own business and invest your money however you'd like. You can invent whatever you want! This nation's support for the innovative and entrepreneurial spirit is rare, indeed.

- You have convenience. Your roads aren't covered with potholes and herds of cattle. You can fly nearly anywhere in the world with only 2-3 layovers. You have maps. Your trash is picked up weekly. Your mail arrives daily. You can watch a YouTube video and learn how to do it yourself in 15 minutes. You have heat and an air-conditioner. Your freezer makes ice. Your bare feet are comfortable on carpet.

I could go on and on, but I think you're getting the point. If you have a pet, your little cat or dog or fish lives a more comfortable, convenient, safe, and reliable life than billions of people will ever know. I'm not trying to make you feel guilty for what you have — I simply want to help you understand that at the root of what you have is where you were born. So, as you enjoy living in the land of opportunity, remember that life is not about what you have, but instead, what you do with what's been given to you for the good of others.

CHAPTER 12

Participation Trophies

"What separates privilege from entitlement is gratitude." — Brene Brown

True entitlement is the fact of having a right to something. For example, if I get strep throat, I am entitled to sick days that give me a right to stay on my couch all day with crackers and watch Netflix. But, the entitlement I'm writing about is the belief that one inherently deserves privileges or special treatment. Yes, this chapter on entitlement strategically follows the chapter, "Born into Privilege." Hopefully this chapter will help you avoid an irrational sense of entitlement — a diagnosis that won't kill you, but it will cause you to believe that you deserve everything in the world for doing absolutely nothing at all.

When I was growing up playing baseball and basketball, if you were terrible, you were terrible…and everyone knew it. If your record at the end of the season was 4 wins and 12 losses, you went home empty-handed. Today, if you stand in right field and pick your nose while your team gets slaughtered, you still get to run off the field and take a picture with your participation trophy. Unfortunately, there are so many parents who simply don't get it. They cheer like their kid is the childhood version of

Kevin Durant, Tom Brady, Lionel Messi, or Tiger Woods, while other parents are watching and secretly wishing that *that kid* would join another team next season. Or, for the love, just quit.

Participation trophies don't work in life. If you don't go to class, you won't be handed a degree. If you don't pay your rent, you'll be handed an eviction notice. If you don't show up for work, you'll be handed a pink slip. If you don't faithfully love your spouse, you'll be handed divorce papers from an attorney. Life isn't like a game in which all participants are handed a trophy. Instead, life can hand you a punch in the face. And trust me, life can hit hard.

The best way to avoid becoming an entitled little brat is to feel and express gratitude. Be grateful for the opportunity to go to college. Be grateful for those who helped you get there. Be grateful for an apartment that you get to call home for the next few years. Be grateful for your roommates. Be grateful for the chance to work and make money. Be grateful for relationships. For parents and professors and police officers and pastors. Be grateful for anyone and anything that helps you get along in life! And then, express that gratitude.

Literally. Move your upper and lower lips, engage your diaphragm, activate your vocal cords, and speak. Try it. Don't just think grateful thoughts. Speak them to those that deserve them. Getting in the habit of sincerely saying *thank you* will set you on a course far away from the land of entitlement. Freedom from entitlement begins with gratitude.

PART TWO
GROW UP

Technically speaking, you are an "adolescent" until the age of nineteen. This is a period of maximum risk and maximum vulnerability according to scientists, which explains why those who carelessly experiment with drugs, alcohol, and sex do so fully focused on pleasure while totally oblivious about potential consequences. And now our culture is attempting to stretch the period of adolescence all the way to 24-years-old. If you're asking me, this is perfect evidence that our culture is undoubtedly guilty of infantilizing your generation. Now, I know what you're thinking: *"What in the world does infantilizing mean?"* I'm glad you asked.

In·fan·til·ize (transitive verb): to keep from maturing; to treat as a baby.

I'm sorry to admit, this is precisely what our tolerant culture is doing. It is acceptable and normal for young people today to sit on the couch and play video games all day rather than work part-time. It is acceptable and normal for young people today to have casual sex and become pregnant, and have an abortion rather than take responsibility and raise the child. It is acceptable and normal for young people today to stay on mommy and daddy's health insurance until their mid-20's and to call AAA rather than learn how to change a flat tire. I've met countless college students who didn't know how to pay a bill or tie a necktie. I've met many others who didn't know how much to tip at a restaurant or which fork to use in a formal dining setting. If you can relate, I suppose part of your *growing pains* is reading this book and me telling you to grow up. And grow up now. Friend, you don't want to look up ten years from now and have no job, no money in the bank, no sense of purpose, and no promising signs of a prosperous future.

Studies show that college education is taking longer, inevitably delaying marriage, parenthood, careers, and financial responsibility. Susan Sawyer, Director of the Center for Adolescent Health at Royal Children's Hospital, claims, *"Although many adult legal privileges start at the age of 18 years, the adoption of adult roles and responsibilities generally occurs later."* History proves that adolescence (a concept that wasn't even recognized until the late 18th Century) isn't something to be proud of. A few hundred years ago, 15-year-old kids *weren't kids.* They were young adults. They worked. They married. They had children. They had grown up.

Without a doubt, the next few years of your life will inevitably include *growing pains.* But for crying out loud, please don't become a casualty of our infantilizing culture. I double dare you — have fun in college, but don't graduate as an adolescent. That would just be embarrassing. Instead, when you graduate and look in the mirror, I hope you are looking into the eyes of a young adult.

CHAPTER 13

Independence

"Sometimes you just gotta be drop-kicked out of the nest." — Robert Downey Jr.

I'm sort of a nature nerd. I love animals and the outdoors. When I was little, I wanted to be a Marine Biologist. I didn't care what the salary or hours looked like, I just wanted to swim around with orca whales and manatees (but not sharks). Even today, trips to the zoo with my four kids are selfishly motivated — I love it. And we pay for an annual family membership to the local aquarium because of me. My wife quickly learned of my infatuation with animals, so for Christmas one year, she gave me a DVD set of the "Planet Earth" television series. Wife of the Year!

In my binge watching of this DVD set, I was fascinated by the research on the snow leopard. These beautiful cats live in the mountains of central Asia, and only a few thousand remain in the wild. They live solitary lives, with only 2-3 living in the same 40 square miles (an area the size of Buffalo, New York). At only 18-22 months old, cubs become completely independent of their mothers. *Independent cubs.* At 18-22 months old, you and I were still pooping in our pants, sleeping in a crib, and sucking on a pacifier. We were barely learning to say "daddy" and "bottle" while snow leopard cubs at that age are forced to stalk and hunt their own food.

The separation between mother and child in the animal kingdom is fascinating. As if the snow leopard relationship seems to be terminated too early, the mommy bunny rabbit visits her young for only a couple of minutes each day, and only for a month. And the most savage of all is the harp seal. The mommy seal feeds her young for about twelve days after labor and delivery. Then, peace out, youngster. Like, how is an abandoned 12-day-old seal supposed to outswim a shark?

On the contrary, one of the most heart-warming mother and child relationships in the animal kingdom is that of the orangutan. Together for 8-9 years, the orangutan mother teaches her child where to find food, what and how to eat, how to detect and avoid predators, and how to build a nest. Female orangutans have been seen visiting their mothers until they are in their mid-teen years, while human teenagers think their mommies are dumb and avoid them at all costs. *We have much to learn from the orangutan.*

I don't know what your mommy is like: a snow leopard, bunny rabbit, harp seal or orangutan. Or maybe your mom isn't present. I've had students whose mothers had passed away, or were consumed by addiction, incarcerated, or too drunk to care. Without knowing your context and upbringing, I do know your path to independence will probably feel exhilarating and terrifying. The average college freshman is mostly or totally dependent on his or her parent's financial support. Many carry a credit card with their daddy's name on it. Most are driving a car that is paid for by mom and dad. Have a random question? Call dad. Having an awful day? Call mom. If you're attending college in your hometown (or within a 90 minute drive from home), you'll probably end up at many Sunday afternoon family

lunches with loads of laundry to be washed and folded by…
guess who…your mom.

All that to say, most college freshmen think they are totally independent on freshman move-in day. However, independence is gradually achieved. Don't delay it (because you're lazy and entitled) and don't rush it (because you're stubborn and prideful). What can you learn from Planet Earth? Don't stay in the nest too long, but don't leave it too soon.

CHAPTER 14

Homesickness

"We don't call it homesick. We call it missing
home. There's not a sickness involved.
It's a state of mind." — John Litten

Do you remember the first time you spent the night away from your home? I'm not talking about your grandmother's house — that doesn't count. I'm talking about the first time your friend from elementary school asked you to sleep over. One of my elementary classmates and youth basketball teammates, Matt, was the first to generously offer me a sleepover opportunity. The invitation felt like one of the criteria that would help mature me toward adulthood. I confidently accepted.

My memories are vague, but we ate a huge dinner, played intense war games with Nerf guns, and eventually landed comfortably in the living room with a bowl of popcorn and a movie. So far, so good. Then it was bedtime. When Matt's mom tucked me into my blankets on the living-room floor, I was internally troubled.

Why? Because Matt's mom, although she was a lovely lady and gracious host, wasn't my mom. And that bed wasn't my bed. I wanted my mom and my bed.

I was ready to be away from home until I was away from

home, and then I wasn't ready to be away from home anymore. I'm not embarrassed to admit what happened next, because you've done something similar. I told Matt's mommy that I felt sick to my stomach. I brilliantly launched my homecoming mission. *"It must have been the popcorn,"* I cried (and lied). She called my mommy and we exchanged a heated dialogue. I knew my mom was already in bed, enjoying a "night off" from, well, me. After convincing her that I was probably going to die from gastroenteritis and irritable bowel syndrome, my mom saved the day (or night). Within half an hour, my mom tucked into my own bed, and interestingly, my stomach didn't hurt anymore. She didn't just save the day. She saved my life.

Author Anthony Brandt says, "Other things may change us, but we start and end with family." I couldn't agree more. Your family is responsible for giving you life (sorry to remind you, but you are alive because your mom and dad "wrestled" under the sheets). Someone in your family changed your nasty diapers and brought you soup in bed when you were sick. They put cash under your pillow when you lost a tooth. Your family drove you to all of your practices and stood in the rain at your soccer games (and pretended to enjoy it). In middle school, your family convinced you of your beauty when your face was covered with pimples. They drove you to the orthodontist after the bubblegum broke a bracket on your braces. They stayed up late helping with your science project and impossible algebra homework. Your family poured peroxide on your knee the first time you fell off your bike and picked up the pieces the first time your heart was broken.

I hope you miss home, *at least a little*. If you don't (and your family qualifies as somewhat normal and caring), you may need to check your heart. Even if you are disappointed in your family of origin, I hope you can give them the benefit of the doubt. *Maybe they tried their hardest and did the best they could.* Odds are, if you're off to college, they did something right. So, in order for you to do something right, here are a few very tangible words of advice concerning your family life:

- Put Father's Day and Mother's Day in your calendar and don't forget them!
- If you don't already know, figure out your parent's birthdays now. Celebrate them. A hand written note or a weekend visit is probably what they'd enjoy the most.
- Your parents want to hear your voice. Don't just text.
- If you have younger siblings, call them at least once a month just to say hello. Check on them. Ask how school and sports are going.
- Visit home. And when you do, don't be a bum and sleep the whole time.
- Don't be an idiot with your parent's money (more in Part 4).
- Do not, under any circumstance, lie to your parents. Explaining why you lied and apologizing is much harder than telling the truth in the first place.

CHAPTER 15

Work Ethic

"You can't have a million dollar dream with a minimum wage work ethic." — Stephen Hogan

My college roommate, Justen, taught me something about excellence. We shared a piece-of-junk apartment east of campus and felt ripped off every month when we paid rent. We actually walked each month to the landlord's office to turn in our check *(yes, we used to write checks back then)*, and it was a miserable walk each time. Honestly, this place was such a dump, *they should have paid us* to live there. Yet, Justen took care of it. He kept dishes clean. He dusted the countertops. He scrubbed the toilet and shower. He vacuumed the carpet. He took out the trash. He even enhanced the aroma of our apartment by burning seasonal candles. My favorite was Christmas time when he lit up the cinnamon candle. I'm telling you, walking from my car to the door, I felt embarrassed to live there. But walking inside our apartment was like being welcomed to my room at the Ritz Carlton. Eventually, I contributed and happily split the chores with Justen.

Your work ethic is important. Hard work is honorable. There is some truth to the principle of "work smart, not hard," like using a dolly to move furniture instead of breaking your back. But goodness, it will serve you well to learn how to work hard. Don't buy into cutting corners, doing a sloppy, mediocre job that lacks attention to detail. Dust the countertops! Trust me — laziness is hard to disguise, and it is very unattractive and unimpressive.

An honorable, admirable work ethic is something you should learn in college. Sure, you're probably not working 40-50 hours every week and the beginning of your career is still many semesters away. But still, with your classwork, involvement with campus activities, and possibly a part-time job, here are some characteristics of a positive work ethic you can put into practice:

- Professionalism *(Conduct yourself in a mature and respectable manner)*
- Excellence *(Don't settle for status quo)*
- Punctuality *(Be on time, which is actually 10 minutes early)*
- Determination *(Be motivated to succeed and go beyond what is expected)*
- Organization *(Be clean and concise; keep a schedule)*
- Cooperation *(Work well with others and be courteous to others)*
- Consistency *(High-quality work isn't occasional, but the norm)*
- Flexibility *(Accommodate unexpected changes or requests)*
- Humility *(Be teachable; ask questions and learn from others)*

CHAPTER 16

Busyness

*"Busyness kills more Christians than
bullets."* — Kevin DeYoung

You might be a busy person. You might not be. You might think you're busy, and you're not. I don't know how you spend your time, but I do know time management is critical to your success in college, relationships, and career.

If I gave you a debit card to an account that holds $161,280, you would probably pee your pants. But here's the catch: you have to spend it in the next 16 weeks. After 16 weeks, any dollars you haven't spent, you lose. I guarantee that you would withdraw and spend every penny. There's no way you would allow a single cent to go to waste! Assuming a semester is 16 weeks long, that means you have 161,280 minutes to spend this spring or fall. And as you already know, every second that ticks by is a second you can't get back. Your cell phone plan may have rollover minutes, but life doesn't. So why do we waste so much time?

There are many arenas competing for your time. Going to class, reading, studying, writing papers, working out, intramurals, visiting home, dating, friendships, road trips, ball games, video games, shopping, working, praying, social media, doing laundry, sleeping, and okay, you get the point. It seems like there simply isn't enough time in the day, right?

Time is a precious gift, and yet we misuse it, waste it, abuse it, undervalue it, and mismanage it. Oswald Sanders says, *"Our problem is not too little time, but making better use of the time we have. Each of us has as much time as anyone else. The President of the United States has the same twenty-four hours as we. Others may surpass our abilities, influence, or money, but no one has more time."*[12]

How do we make better use of our time? Fight busyness. I encourage you, build a life that is *full*, not busy. Don't get addicted to the drug of busyness. Learn now to put your feet up and rest. I'm not encouraging laziness. I'm encouraging you to sit still every once in a while. And by the way, if you think you're busy now, just wait. You'll really be forced to learn time management in order to juggle a marriage, children, a career, and activities for the family every evening of the week!

Here is a trick that I learned over the years that I'd encourage you to apply. Break your calendar down to 21 different blocks of time: morning, afternoon and evening on all 7 days. Write in your commitments that take the majority of your time in the blocks. In the following example, I've filled in what a college student's schedule could look like. The ultimate goal I'm suggesting is that your schedule maintains 4 open blocks *(roughly 20% of your time)*. These "OPEN" blocks don't represent time that you lay on the couch like a lazy slob, but instead, time that you can choose how to spend *productively*.

Day	Morning	Afternoon	Evening
Monday	Class, 8am-12pm	Class, 1pm-4pm	Work, 6pm-10pm
Tuesday	Class, 8am-12pm	**OPEN**	Work, 6pm-10pm
Wednesday	Class, 8am-12pm	Class, 1pm-4pm	Time with Friends
Thursday	Class, 8am-12pm	Work, 1pm-6pm	**OPEN**
Friday	Class, 8am-12pm	**OPEN**	Work, 6pm-10pm
Saturday	Sleep in	Tailgating	Football Game
Sunday	Church	**OPEN**	Study, 6pm-10pm

CHAPTER 17

Sleep

"I love sleep. My life has the tendency to fall apart when I'm awake." — Ernest Hemingway

Maybe you noticed in the previous chapter, the calendar has Saturday morning designated for sleeping in. Also notice: the calendar does not specify any other mornings as a time to stay in bed and waste a third of a day. Realistically, I know you need one morning to hit the snooze button, or not even set an alarm clock the night before. But other than one morning each week, get your tail out of bed!

You've heard the saying, "The early bird gets the worm." You may think, *"Who cares, I don't want a stupid worm – I'll get up much later and have a bowl of Frosted Flakes."* You might be the kind of person who could be a "morning person," if morning happened around noon. It's bizarre — many students crave sleep in the mornings, are dying to sleep in the afternoons, and refuse to sleep at night.

I implore you – don't sleep 10 hours every day. If you do, you'll sleep through 41.6% of your college years. Every single day is full of opportunity! Don't miss out because you can't peel yourself off of your pillow. Go to bed at a decent hour (2:30am after multiple hours of watching Netflix or playing video games is not a decent hour). Set an alarm, get up and go! Carpe diem!

CHAPTER 18

Diet and Exercise

*"You can't exercise your way out of
a bad diet."* — Mark Hyman

You've probably heard jokes (or been warned) about the "Freshman 15." These are the 15 pounds that many students gain during their first year of college. This typically happens due to unhealthy eating, excessive drinking, or simply sitting around being lazy. Maybe I'm the first to tell you, you don't have to eat unhealthy, drink excessively, or sit around doing nothing just because you left home and went to college.

Most colleges and universities include a membership to a fitness center on campus. I remember one student telling me he didn't exercise because he didn't have a car to get to the fitness center. I thought...*bro, you live on campus...jog to the gym!* At the end of the day, no one can keep you in shape (or get you in shape) but you. You can make excuses all day long, or you can make an effort. As for your diet, here are some practical tips to staying healthy in college:

1. Eat breakfast. This kick-starts your metabolism.
2. Eat proper portion sizes. A large pizza to yourself is not proper.

3. Eat early. 10pm dinners are not going to digest very quickly.
4. Eat healthy. Not just your meals, but also your snacks. Apples, not Cheetos.
5. Eat in control. Don't turn to food when you're stressed. Instead, go for a run.
6. Drink water. Pack a water bottle for class and stay hydrated.
7. Drink moderately. If you're 21-years-old, and you are going to drink beer, remember that they range from 100-150 calories per can. Even if your normal dinner is grilled chicken and sautéed vegetables, drinking 4-5 beers in one night is the equivalent of two cheeseburgers.
8. Drink caffeine when you need it. Not just because it's available.
9. Take a multi-vitamin. A nutritional supplement will help your diet, your concentration, and can even help you avoid common illnesses.

Burgers and tacos can land you in a really unhealthy lifestyle that you'll struggle to reverse later in adulthood. However, some young people enter college with the desire to attain the perfect body and end up practicing diet and exercise in very unhealthy ways. A study on college student's diet and exercise behaviors provided disheartening results. Out of 302 students who participated in the study, 50% of students who were rated underweight on the basis of their BMI (Body-Mass Index) classified themselves as overweight.[13] Translation: people who were a healthy weight *felt* overweight. This is not surprising when you consider our airbrush-dependent culture. Despite what you see on magazines and in movies, the perfect body is a healthy body — not overweight, not underweight.

Ecclesiastes 9:7 encourages us to eat our food with gladness. However, food has become a sensitive issue in our society. Many young people struggle with eating disorders. For the sake of specificity, here are the three most common disorders relating to food:

- Anorexia — people who generally view themselves as overweight, even if they're dangerously underweight; includes a relentless pursuit of thinness and unwillingness to maintain a healthy weight.
- Bulimia — people who frequently eat unusually large amounts of food in a relatively short period. After painfully feeling full, individuals will attempt to purge to compensate for the calories they consumed (including forced vomiting, fasting, laxatives and excessive exercise).
- Binge Eating — people who frequently eat unusually large amounts of food in a relatively short period and do not restrict calories. Individuals eat uncontrollably, even when they are not hungry.

I sincerely hope you will experience a healthy lifestyle in college. But if you currently struggle with an eating disorder, please put this book down and call the **National Eating Disorders Association Helpline: 1-800-931-2237.**

CHAPTER 19

Current Events

*"If you don't vote, you lose the right
to complain."* — George Carlin

Did you know that you could vote? As a citizen, you can join others and decide who deserves the titles of Mayor, Governor, Judge and President of the United States. One of the most significant events in our nation happens every couple of years. New candidates start to campaign and cast their vision. Look into the political climate around you, register to vote, and then show up to the polls.

It is time for you to care about what is happening across this country and the world, too. Look beyond your campus bubble and your zip code. On your social media, don't just follow your friends and favorite celebrities. Find and follow multiple sources for news and check into the world a little bit more than you currently are. Do you know what laws are being voted on in your state? Do you know what the weather is supposed to look like next week? What challenges is your community facing? What social injustices are nearby and how can you be an advocate for change? Where is Iran on a map? What are the top five religions in the world? What is the current natural disaster impacting an entire region? Who is our Vice President? How much is the American dollar worth in Europe? What are the primary conflicts in the world? What is our military up to? What is an Amber Alert? A Silver Alert?

I'll admit, current events can feel a bit depressing. I mean, watching or reading the news drops my jaw to the ground in disbelief. But still. You simply should *be aware* of current events in the world, you should *care about* current events in the world, and even if you don't care, you need to be able to hang in conversations about current events to avoid looking like a complete, uninformed idiot. Ultimately, you should know about current events in the world because it is the world you live in. If you don't already, it is time to start caring about your neighbors, both near and far.

CHAPTER 20

The Campus Bubble

"It's a big world, and I really like it." — George Saunders

I knew college students who never left their campus. I'm not kidding. Ok, maybe they went home for Thanksgiving and Christmas, but other than that, they lived like little hermits. The invisible walls of your campus will inevitably start to feel like a bubble, and staying inside is easy and comfortable. I had college students who didn't come to church because it was a 7-mile drive from campus. When I reminded them that the round trip drive would only cost $1.25 in gas, they'd tell me they didn't want to move their car and lose their spot in the parking lot. Lazy bums.

You need to leave campus. Trust me. There's only so much you can do and learn and accomplish within the square mile of your dorm, library, and classrooms. If you ask me, staying put seems mundane. Hopefully you know of life happening outside of your campus bubble and have a little fear of missing out. There are experiences to have, things to discover and opportunities to learn and grow outside of your college campus. Visit home more often. Work off campus. Move off campus. Study abroad. There is indeed a great big world out there and you don't have to wait until retirement to see and experience it.

CHAPTER 21

Protect Your Identity

*"Your identity is your most valuable possession.
Protect it."* — Elastigirl (The Incredibles)

In your first 30 days of college, you'll be invited to sign up for 30 different credit cards. They'll promise you a cool t-shirt if you'll fill out a form and write down your social security number *(by the way, you need to memorize your SSN if you haven't already).* You probably packed 100 shirts for college. You don't need one more, and you certainly don't need to be writing your most sensitive information on some inexperienced salesman's clipboard at a New Student Orientation Fair. According to the U.S. Department of Justice, 1 in 7 U.S. residents will be a victim of identity theft. This is a rising problem in society, and you can do a few things to prevent becoming an unfortunate victim.

Keep your mail safe. If it has your information written anywhere, don't leave it lying around, and certainly don't throw it away as is. Shred that puppy into 1,000 pieces. With your credit/debit cards, check the statements frequently and read all of the charges to ensure there aren't purchases that you don't recognize.

I know you probably trust your roommate, but do you know all the people he or she will bring home? *Probably not.*

Set a password on your phone and laptop so that if you walk away, someone can't open your apps or Internet and steal your information. Oh, and don't set your password as "1234567890" like I used to. Know where your wallet or purse is at all times and don't leave it in your car overnight.

Lastly, for your personal safety, be careful to never reveal your address on your social media accounts. Surely you'd never post the actual physical address online, but photographs can reveal what apartment complex you live in or where you spent a good deal of time. Stalkers pay attention to these kinds of things. Let me offer a worst-case scenario:

A total creep spots you at a party and finds out your name.

He searches, finds and follows you on social media.

You post a picture with your friends at your apartment swimming pool.

He researches local apartment complexes online and finds the pool.

He waits at the pool multiple days in a row until you need some sun.

He watches to see what apartment building you head home to.

He waits patiently. You post on Facebook: *"Roommate is out of town. Enjoying some alone time."* He pays you a surprise visit. You open the door. And, your mom and dad get a horrifying phone call from the local police with the very worst news any parent could ever hear.

I know, you're wondering why this chapter is ending with a horror story. Sorry. *But not sorry.* I have three daughters and I think about their safety every day. I will do my best to teach them how to be safe when they leave for college, and want to warn you as well. All I'm saying is this: be careful.

PART THREE
ACADEMICS

Everyone knows you have to study in order to graduate college. Have you ever noticed that the act of *studying* ends with the letters "dying?" Stu*dying*. It is one of the least enjoyable features of college, and it usually demands your attention at the most inconvenient times.

I remember a class I took my senior year, and 20% of our final grade reflected our verbal interaction with the professor after his lectures. Following lectures that I barely understood, I had to come up with a thought-provoking question to ask this brilliant professor. The hope is that he would think that I was somewhat comprehending what he was talking about. Not only was the pressure to come up with a stimulating question completely unbearable, but I also worried that my classmates would read right through me and know I was a fraud. After doing my best to craft the perfect question, I'd raise my hand and wait to be called on. My heart raced. Then, he'd look at me. "Yes, Adam?" This was my moment.

> *"Professor, I'm fascinated by the modern influences of Plato, Aristotle and Kant, but in the history of ethics, can you help me understand blah, blah, blah... as well as why they blah, blah, blah?"*

It was the effort that counted. I passed the class, but in that particular course, my motto was *fake it till I make it.*

In college, you'll be expected to visit your school's library and understand how to hunt down multiple sources. You'll take quizzes and exams and midterms and finals. You'll work with groups on assignments, and, without a doubt, there will be one group member that couldn't care less and doesn't contribute squat, but then shows up for the class presentation and takes all the credit. You'll fall asleep in class and miss deadlines for assignments. You'll write papers and right-click thousands of words, scroll down to "synonyms," and click more impressive (and lengthier) words. You'll calculate the exact score you need on a final exam in order to make a B- in a class. You'll probably beg a professor for extra credit opportunities. Your academic career might be a ton of fun or a pain in the neck, or both. Either way, stay committed. Work hard. Finish.

CHAPTER 22

GPA

"Finals Week Motto: C's get Degrees."
— Millions of College Students

Dad: *"So how is your GPA this semester?"*
You: *"Well, dad, the good thing is that we have our health."*
There are many factors that contribute to calculating your GPA. Certainly it reflects the amount of points you score on assignments, papers, and tests, but also included is how late you stay up, your social life, your study habits, and how much you actually care.

Without a doubt, your GPA matters significantly when trying to land your first job after college, as it will represent your work ethic, intelligence, commitment level, and competence. Your GPA also matters to your parents' right this very moment, especially if they're paying your bursar account balance. If you let your GPA dip for some reason over the course of a semester, you better make some immediate changes. Don't sit around and twirl your thumbs while your GPA plummets. You are the only one that can take the steps to improve, so take responsibility, create an action plan, and keep your eye on the prize.

Part of maintaining an impressive GPA is reaching out for help. Your professors are not monsters and tutors are not a waste of time or money. Take advantage of your library and academic center on campus. Get involved with study groups. Break the ice with your Teacher's Assistant by honestly admitting, "I have no idea what I'm doing." You'll find that professionals in the academic world are much more patient and understanding than their syllabus ever conveys.

CHAPTER 23

Switching Majors

"Change is hard at first, messy in the middle, and gorgeous in the end." — Robin Sharma

When I was beginning my college career, I originally launched into the direction of medicine and wanted to become a neonatal pediatrician. I had dreams of living my life in a white coat and saving thousands of babies' lives. And then, I started to study anatomy and realized that blood and guts weren't my things. I mean, I can clean a fish without gagging, but the thought of making an incision on the human epidermis with a scalpel makes me want to throw up. So, I changed my major.

According to the U.S. Department of Education, roughly one-third of college students change their major at least one time. And get this: half of all students whose originally declared major was mathematics switched majors within three years.[14] If you find yourself unsettled in the path you're on, talk to your parents and your advisor. Assess your goals and try to imagine your life in the career path you've chosen. Do some research and explore other majors that seem appealing to you.

While changing your major is very normal, it should be treated as a very delicate decision. Doing so can require an extra semester or two of classes (which obviously increases the cost of your education), and can also delay your career path. The longer it takes you to decide on a direction, and the more times you change your major, the more likely you'll aimlessly walk through your twenties trying to figure out just what you want to do. Do your best to land on an area of study that represents your passions and your goals in life.

After college, you are statistically likely to change paths as an adult, too. According to the Bureau of Labor Statistics, the Baby Boomer generation held an average of 11.7 jobs from the ages of 18 to 48.[15] For many, that meant packing up a house and relocating multiple times! Very rarely do adults remain in the same job their entire career. So don't be alarmed or afraid: change is coming, probably in college and maybe in adulthood.

CHAPTER 24

The Need to Read

"Read to refill the wells of inspiration."
— Harold Ockenga

I heard about a man who was so obsessed with reading that he took a suitcase full of books on his honeymoon. One could argue that his obsession was a bit overboard. I've only been on one honeymoon myself, and there was no time for reading if you get my drift.

I encourage you to read and not just the books you're assigned to read for class. Cultivate the discipline of reading for pleasure. Read to learn. Read to grow. Read to discover. You might be rolling your eyes and thinking I'm out of my mind, as all of your reading assignments in high school were painfully boring to you. You'd rather watch paint dry.

You were probably forced to pick up *The Scarlett Letter* or *To Kill a Mockingbird* in recent years. I encourage you to pick up something to read, not because you are forced by a syllabus, but because you are intrigued. There are so many genres of literature out there. Think for a moment if any of these interest you:

- Science fiction
- Satire

- Drama
- Action and Adventure
- Romance
- Mystery
- Horror
- Self-Help
- Health
- Travel
- Spirituality
- Science
- History
- Poetry
- Comics
- Art
- Biographies
- Autobiographies

I always have a book in my car in case I have time to kill. Trust me, scrolling your thumbs on your phone is such a waste of time compared to gazing your eyes on the pages of a good book. Dr. Seuss said it best: *"The more that you read, the more things you will know. The more that you know, the more places you'll go."*

CHAPTER 25

Procrastination

"Have you something to do tomorrow?
Do it today." — Benjamin Franklin

When I was in college, I went skydiving with a bunch of friends. I remember acting cool, calm and collected on the outside, but I was panicking on the inside. During our training session, I remember asking the instructor if any of his customers had ever died. When he let out a casual, *"yup,"* my stomach knotted up and I nearly peed my pants.

While jumping out of an airplane has got to be one of my dumbest decisions ever, I'm so glad I did it. I'll never forget the sensation of rolling out of the airplane and doing front flips all the way down. Clouds. Ground. Clouds. Ground. Clouds. Ground. And then came the pulling of the cord, which released my one hope of living another day. As the parachute spread out and caught air, my descent slowed down and I was able to take in the breathtaking view and extraordinary sensation of floating in mid-air. I also remember pulling the cord and then experiencing what felt like a vicious kick to the crotch. But, I suppose you want the harness as tight as possible when you're falling from 10,000 feet at 125mph.

The timing of pulling the cord is critical, and it *can happen* too late. Obviously, pulling a parachute cord too late and turning in an English paper too late is kind of an unfair comparison with entirely different consequences. However, I'm trying to sell you on this point: don't procrastinate.

Procrastination is a thief of time, and as Oswald Sanders says, "One of the devil's most potent weapons."[16] Academically, unnecessary delays in reading, studying, and writing will wipe you out one credit at a time. The goal for a college student is to stay slightly ahead of your tasks rather than always trying to catch up. Like so many other times in this book, I'll remind you that this is something to get under control *now*, as your spouse, children, boss, and mortgage company won't be so forgiving if your tendency to procrastinate continues post-college.

Get organized, keep a calendar, make a plan, set alarms and deadlines, prioritize, sacrifice, pace yourself, and take breaks. If you do, you'll get it done, and you'll get it done on time (or even better, early).

CHAPTER 26

The Family Business

"Your potential is endless. Go do what you were created to do." — Sarah Lopez

When my wife and I visited the Vatican and walked through the Sistine Chapel, we saw all the signs that said, "No Photography." Confession: I took a couple of photos. I couldn't help it. We were standing in a papal chapel built in the late 1400s. Overhead were nine scenes from the Book of Genesis that were painted by Michelangelo between 1508 and 1512. Most famous, of course, is *The Creation of Adam*. Michelangelo was a sculptor, painter, architect, and poet who is credited for his incomparable influence on the development of western art.

This is a guy that was once found chipping away at a block of marble, and when he was asked what he was carving, he answered, *"I am not carving anything; I am releasing the angel from within the stone."*[17] Really, you have to be an incredibly unique, creative, iconic, imaginative, ingenious human being to think that way, much less, know how to translate your thoughts into words like that!

Michelangelo was born on March 6, 1475 in Caprese, Italy. His father, Lodovico Buonarroti, worked as a government official. Now, let's pretend the following scene unfolded in Michelangelo's childhood:

When young Mike was almost 10-years-old, his father found him in the courtyard one afternoon mixing paint colors with a paintbrush. Lodovico asked him, "Son, what are you painting?" He replied, *"I'm not painting anything; I am releasing the bunny rabbit from within the canvas."* His father raged with anger and screamed: "Mike! The Buonarroti family tree has no artists and we are keeping it that way. You will throw away those paintbrushes and you will follow my footsteps and serve the government." Poor Mike did as his father wished and never picked up a paintbrush again.

There goes *The Creation of Adam* and my photo of the Sistine Chapel.

This *might be* the one chapter of this book that your parents don't want you to read if it directly applies to your context. As a child, hopefully you felt the freedom to express interest in whatever sincerely interested you. You don't have to chase a certain career just because mom and dad have applied unfair and unbearable pressure on you throughout your childhood.

How do you know if you've been pressured to pursue a certain profession? Let's say you've *never expressed any interest in becoming a doctor,* but:

- Your parents bought you a pretend doctor kit every Christmas and forced you to play with a stethoscope, thermometer, blood pressure cuff, forceps, bandages, eyeglasses, a scalpel, tweezers, a syringe, scissors, a reflex hammer, and ear scope.
- Your mom pretended to be your patient and visited your "doctor office" with every ailment known by man.
- Every Halloween, you were dressed up in scrubs.

- When you caught an insect, your dad encouraged you to dissect it.
- Every time you got fever, a cough, a sore throat, or a splinter, your parents rushed you to Urgent Care and introduced you to "your future."

You get the point. You don't have to become something because your parents said so. You don't have to study what they studied. You don't have to run the family business. My father worked as a general contractor and I grew up surrounded by tools and saw dust. I consider myself pretty handy, but still find myself at Home Depot asking really dumb questions. My dad never pressured me to continue the "Barnett Building Company." Plus, he's the best builder on the planet. If I were his succession plan, the company would have imploded. Instead, my dad let me discover my passions and encouraged me along the way.

Friday is a desirable day of the week for people who hate their career. Do what *you love,* and you'll never have a problem with Monday.

CHAPTER 27

Academic Dishonesty

"An Aggie does not lie, cheat or steal or tolerate those who do." — Texas A&M Code of Honor

I graduated from the University of Oklahoma (a Big XII school), so I'm not a fan of the SEC. Yet, I have a lot of respect for the Texas A & M Code of Honor: *"An Aggie does not lie, cheat or steal or tolerate those who do."*[18] I'm warning you, if you cheat in college, you have a very high chance of being caught. And once you're caught, you'll be fumbling your words to come up with a reasonable excuse for an academic dean that doesn't want to hear it. This is serious business and the results of academic dishonesty are not very forgiving.

I remember researching online to collect information for a paper in seminary: "Exegesis of Ephesians 5." As I researched, I remember reading a very powerful article that taught me something brand new, something that I wouldn't soon forget. A few weeks later when we were commenting on classmate's papers, I reviewed a paper that was also on Ephesians 5. While reading this paper, I recognized roughly half of a page of content was from the article that had caught my attention during my own research. I went to her footnotes to see if she had cited the author. *She didn't.* She had copy/pasted an entire section of an online article and used it for her paper, without giving credit to the author. And that was *seminary.*

Plain and simple: don't cheat.

Oh, and by the way, cheating is always wrong. Long after college is over, you're spouse, children, boss, and the IRS won't tolerate it either.

PART FOUR
MONEY

Because a biblical perspective is what I'm most familiar with, let me begin there. Did you know that the topics of generosity and money are mentioned a combined 2,886 times in the Bible? That is 6.8 times more than heaven and hell...*combined*. There are 38 recorded parables taught by Jesus and 16 of them are concerning money and possessions. In the Gospels (Matthew, Mark, Luke and John), 10% of the text deals directly with stewardship and management of resources. The Bible offers roughly 500 verses on prayer, less than 500 verses on faith, but over 2,000 verses on money![19] I believe this frequency is to our advantage, because it offers us direction, counsel, and warning. As a matter of fact, the Bible includes advice on the following: budgeting, earning money, worrying about money, saving, stewardship, business management, giving money, investing, receiving, success, contentment, love of money, planning, lending, financial security, debt, wasting money, tithing, prosperity, and even taxes! Through the Bible, it is made clear that money can be hazardous or helpful.

John D. Rockefeller was at one point the richest man in the world. He was the very first American billionaire. When asked the question, *"How much money is enough?"* he famously answered: *"Just a little bit more."* We could all use just a little more money, right? I can tell you three things I wish I had right now, but it simply wouldn't be wise to spend the money. But money (or the desire for more) can control people so much that they're willing to compromise their integrity, values, relationships, justice, and even life itself. James Patterson, author of *The Day America Told the Truth*, reveals some shocking and disappointing statistics on how far people would go to have more. In one survey, people anonymously answered what they were willing to do for ten million dollars:

- 25% of people said they would abandon their entire family
- 23% of people would become a prostitute for one week
- 21% of people said they would let their spouse have sex with someone else
- 16% of people said they would give up their American citizenship
- 10% of people would withhold their testimony and let a murderer go free
- 7% of people would kill a stranger
- 3% of people would give up their children[20]

I've heard people say that money is a great servant, but a horrible master. The research you just read confirms that being mastered by an unrelenting desire for more money causes people to think like complete lunatics.

I remember graduating college and accepting a full-time ministry position at a church. I made a whopping $22k/year and genuinely felt like I was rolling in the dough. Fifteen years and four children later, I feel like I spend $22,000 per year on soccer tournaments and Chick-Fil-A. As life progresses, we could all use a little more money, but don't let your desire for more change you for the worse.

In the following chapters, let me offer a few ideas and warnings when it comes to your relationship with money (or your desire for more).

CHAPTER 28

Get a Job

"Shut up and get a real job."
— Stephen Barnett (no relation)

If your parents are not helping you with college tuition (because they don't want to or can't afford to) and you have to work your way through college, I applaud you. You are getting an early introduction to "the real world." You can also skip this chapter if you'd like. You probably have to get to work anyway.

If your parents are paying for your college tuition but you have to work to pay your rent, car payment, cell phone bill, etc., I applaud you, too. Be sure to thank your parents often for doing what they can to help.

If your parents are paying your tuition, rent, utilities, cell phone bill, insurance, food, car payment, gas, and so on, this chapter is for you. You should get a job, not because you need the money, but because you need the experience and life lessons. Relax, I'm not telling you to go work 20-30 hours per week. Just get a simple part time job. Be a waiter, a lifeguard, a babysitter, or mow some lawns. Work at the gym, be a substitute teacher for a nearby middle school, or referee for youth soccer. I'm only talking about 2-3 shifts each week — something that will help you prepare for a big boy or big girl job someday. Here are some things you'll learn, even in a part time job:

- People skills (communicate with someone other than your roommate)
- Problem solve (sorry, your parents can't help with problems at work)
- Patience (some jobs can be rather mundane, work hard anyway)
- Tolerance (you'll work with people that drive you completely nuts)
- Flexibility (your duties may change with very little notice)
- Appreciation (you see money differently when you work for it)
- Hard work (to keep a job, you've got to get the job done)
- Time management (staying on task and meeting deadlines)
- Self-control (holding your tongue when your boss is irritating)
- Commitment (because you will have days that tick you off and make you want to quit, but you won't want to quit later in life when you have a wife, children, and a mortgage)

CHAPTER 29

Learn to Budget

"A budget is learning to tell your money where to go instead of learning where it went." — Dave Ramsey

One of the greatest lessons you can learn early about finances is this: don't spend more money than you make! This lesson is mostly ignored not because people love debt, but because they never learn how to budget. Rather than your parents teaching you how to manage money, it is possible that you watched them spend uncontrollably throughout your childhood...like that one year when your dad took a pay cut, yet still bought your mom a new SUV and took the whole family to Disney World. That, my friend, is not the example of budgeting you want to follow.

Right now, your commitments are relatively minimal compared to what your future holds. While you're focused right now on paying for dinner with your friends and filling up your car with gas, one day you'll be looking at a mortgage payment, insurance, property taxes, car repairs, subscriptions, vacations, medical expenses, chiropractor visits, club memberships, Christmas presents, anniversary gifts, and donations to philanthropic organizations that constantly hit you up for money. The older you get, the more ways you can and will spend your money.

I had a friend in college who graduated one year before me. He made just under $40k in the first year of his career. After wrapping up his first year, I'll never forget him telling me, *"I don't have any money left. I don't know what happened."* I'm not judging the guy, but comparing my own situation to his reveals a significant problem. In our first year of marriage, Andrea and I were full time students. We both worked part time and our combined income was just over $26k that year. We had a mortgage payment on our home, a car payment, and all the normal utilities and expenses one incurs after getting married. Even with our limited income, we still could have taken a vacation! Two of us lived off of $26k while our single friend couldn't figure out how $40k disappeared. It all comes back to spending. Budgeting. Self-control. Stewardship.

I'm not going to explain you how to budget. There are plenty of solid financial professionals who can give you the nuts and bolts of successful financial planning and budgeting (see the endnotes for suggestions).[21] I'm simply warning you: the first time you're handed a paycheck (if you haven't received one already), you're going to feel rich, and you can find ways to blow every dime in about 45 minutes. So, be conscious of the fact that learning to budget will cost you some things you *want* right now, but will give you something you *need* down the road: financial peace.

CHAPTER 30

Parents and Plastic

"The most delicious of all privileges is spending other people's money."— John Randolph

You have *no idea* how expensive your childhood was, so I'm going to tell you. Research offers three separate spending levels that your parents may have chosen to apply to your childhood. Let me break down all three:

1. Basic Essentials: food, housing, clothing, transportation, health care, and health insurance. Housing and transportation cost the most, as married couples with a child spend almost $80,000 more on housing than married couples with no kids, and almost $57,000 more on transportation, according to the Bureau of Labor.

2. Deluxe Essentials: all of the above with more expensive choices for food and clothing, and the cost of life insurance for both parents.

3. Deluxe Perks: all of the above, plus extras for early childhood care, college savings, education, music and sports lessons, family vacations, electronics and gaming, and other purchases "just because."

After deciding which category best represents your childhood, here is what your parents spent on you, on average, from conception to college:

Basic essentials: $260,366
Deluxe essentials: $342,976
Deluxe Perks: $745,634[22]

I don't tell you that to make you feel bad or to place a price tag on your upbringing. Instead, I want you to see and understand the financial investment your parents have made over the years to get you to this point. I'm also warning you: don't act entitled and flippantly spend your parent's money throughout college, as if they haven't already given and sacrificed enough! Show some respect. If you have a credit card or debit card that sends a bill to your parents each month, keep in mind that money doesn't grow on trees. They are working hard for that money. Before you swipe the card or insert the chip, ask yourself, *"If someone had my credit card, would I want him or her to spend like this?"*

Another thing: if you flunk a class because you simply don't understand the content and got in way over your head, and you met with your professor for help, and you utilized tutors, and you studied your tail off and turned in all your assignments, and you still flunked — your parents will most likely understand. You gave it your best shot. An honest effort.

If you flunk a class because you slept in, occasionally attended, and failed to study or turn in assignments, you are abusing your parent's finances. That is simply unacceptable and someone should give you a loving backhand slap across the face. Every time I play golf, I think of how much I'm spending per hole. So, if the green fee is $95.00, every hole is worth $5.28. That's not too bad of a deal. But if you apply the same concept to your class schedule, it is amazing to see how much money your parents are spending each time you head to class. If the average cost per credit hour is $594.00, then your three-hour course is worth 1,782.00. If this class meets twice each week (Tuesday/Thursday) over the course of 15 weeks, that's 30 class sessions *(this is high level math, huh?)*. This concludes that each time you go to class, your parents are paying $59.40 to your professor and university. Or another way of putting it: each time you skip a class, you are wasting $59.40 of your parent's money.

Basic essentials, deluxe essentials or deluxe perks, it doesn't really matter. You've been given the opportunity of a lifetime to go to college. Take advantage of the opportunity without taking advantage of your folks.

CHAPTER 31

Debt

"Debt is the slavery of the free." — Publilius Syrus

"Those who want to get rich fall into temptation and a trap and into many foolish and harmful desires that plunge people into ruin and destruction." (1 Timothy 6:9) This verse describes a series of unfortunate events that millions of people experience when it comes to finances. It is called *debt* and here is how it happens:

1. See things you want
2. Need money to purchase what you want
3. Work really hard and make money
4. Purchase things you want
5. See more things you want
6. Spend more money than what you make
7. Accrue debt
8. Self-destruct

You were not created to find fulfillment in the accumulation of stuff. Yet, as financial guru Dave Ramsey puts it, "We buy things we don't need with money we don't have, all to impress people that we don't know." Materialism is a downward spiral, resulting in temporary satisfaction and permanent addiction. Materialism is when you stop possessing things and start letting things possess you. This ought to scare you a little: a ton of people spend more money than they make. And for what? Pleasure? Image? Keeping up with the neighbor's recent purchases? Even worse, I've read a lot of research over the years that link debt to higher probabilities of depression.

There are certain debts people acquire that are understandable. Not everyone can pay cash for a college education or a new home. However, you can control unnecessary debt by resisting the urge to own every new, shiny product or electronic upgrade, or outfit in the window.

One of the greatest words of financial advice I can give you is to have a healthy relationship with credit cards. Because of the way our world is shifting toward plastic, I'm assuming you have a card of some sort. This isn't necessarily a bad thing if you are only putting items on your card that you would purchase with cash (gas and groceries) or online banking (cable, internet, and cell phone bills). As long as you don't lose control and stay disciplined with your budget, swiping the card or inserting the chip isn't necessarily harmful. As a matter of fact, it could be helpful. By using your card for purchases you'd already make with cash or checks, you'll begin building a good credit history. However, you'll only build a good credit history if you pay your credit card statement on time and in full every month.

If you are working part time and paying for your own college tuition, you'll likely need to apply for student loans. This is a widely accepted and understandable form of debt; however, please apply for scholarships, too. Last year alone, United States high school seniors who were eligible to receive Pell Grants, but neglected to complete a FAFSA

(Free Application for Federal Student Aid), missed out on $2.9 billion in scholarships.[23] That's $2,955,475,413 to be exact. Who knows, there might be some cash out there waiting on you, and all it would take is a 30-minute application. Give it a try and see what happens!

CHAPTER 32

Poverty Mentality

"I am not poor. Poor are those who desire many things." — Leonardo da Vinci

In 2010, we flew to the Philippines with our 10-month-old daughter, Ellie, and eight others for what would be an unforgettable trip. Sure, there are plenty of great memories we shared together, but something happened that still bothers me today: we were robbed. My backpack was stolen, which possessed our passports, $4,500 in cash, our room key, my favorite pocketknife, my Bible, and of course, candy. There we were, 8,207 miles from home with no identification, no money, and no candy. The next few days were somewhat of a blur, as I was on the phone for countless hours and had to fill out a never-ending stack of paperwork. We declared our passports as stolen, flew to Manila to receive our temporary travel documents from the U.S. Embassy, and put the pieces together to get home safely.

In the moment, I felt somewhat hopeless. Over the years, the event occasionally crosses my mind, and as my grandmother would say, it makes me "madder than a hornet." I can't really fathom the thought of stealing from someone else, but then I remember that some people are simply that desperate. The amount of money in my backpack that day was equivalent to the average *annual* income in the Philippines. Correct. I carried an entire year's salary on my back. Pretty dumb. I'm surprised I wasn't robbed sooner.

What ticks me off more than being robbed in the Philippines is hearing a college student claim he or she is poor. For a little perspective, the average starting salary for Class of 2018 business majors is $51,872.[24]

Earning more than $25,000 per year places you in the top 10% of the world's income earners. Earning $50,000 or more annually (the average starting salary previously mentioned), you are in the top 1% of the world's income earners. And if you have any money saved or drove a car to college, you are in the top 5% of the world's wealth.[25]

Speaking of cars, have you heard the story of the wealthy man who had a very bad car accident? He was driving his BMW to the golf course and never saw the other car coming. His car was completely totaled. The first policeman to arrive to the scene rushed to help the man, pulling him out from the window, as the door was completely smashed in. He was significantly injured and a bit disoriented, but still began to cry, *"Oh, no! My BMW! My beautiful BMW!"* This completely shocked the policeman, who replied, *"Sir, that is the least of your worries. Your arm has been severed at the elbow."* The wealthy man, now aware that he had lost his arm in the accident, cried even louder, *"Oh, no! My Rolex!"*

You have to admit, that is funny. But it is also revealing of the priorities of many people who worry about their expensive cars and accessories, while three billion people live on less than $2.00 per day. All that to say, please don't think, speak, or act like you are poor, as you will likely have and consume more than half of the people on this planet over the course of your life.

CHAPTER 33

Generosity

"It isn't our money, Adam. Its God's money.
So don't be stingy." — Andrea Barnett

I am convinced that no one on their deathbed says, *"I wish I would have given less to others."* At some point in our lives, we wake up and realize that it is more of a blessing to give than to receive (see Acts 20:35). Fortunately, I've learned this lesson, but I learned it the hard way. For years, I lived with an insanely selfish mindset. Unfortunately, my greed crushed my wife's heart. Let me explain.

Early in our marriage, before we had children, we spent a lot of time in the Oklahoma City Rescue Mission. This shelter provides three warm meals and a place to sleep for thousands of homeless people every day. One day, Andrea learned about a homeless woman who had a baby. *So what do you think she did?* She went to Target. That night, glowing with excitement, she told me everything she purchased for this homeless mother. The conversation looked like this:

Andrea: *"I met a young woman today at the shelter who had a baby!"*

Me: *"That's wonderful, sweetheart! I'm so glad you were a friend to her."*

Andrea: *"Me too! I went to Target and got some things for her and the baby!"*

Me: *"What did you get?"* (I was totally hoping to hear only 2-3 items)

Andrea: *"Burp rags, diapers, pacifiers, clothes... babe, I filled the cart!"*

Selfish Me: *"You filled the cart?"*

My comment changed the mood of our conversation very quickly. After a few moments of awkward silence, you could guess what I asked her next...

"How much did you spend?" Just so you know, I'm not proud to write this. Ridiculous, isn't it? In hindsight, I'm embarrassed to know that as a young man, husband and pastor, I was all about serving the homeless with my time and energy, but not my money.

I stole Andrea's joy that day. And that was the day that I began to learn what radical generosity looks like. I'm so thankful to God for giving me "Mrs. Generosity" as a bride. In all my years of marriage, I've never seen one situation in which Andrea has been greedy. I'm serious, NOT ONE. Through her example and God's patience, I've learned that our checkbooks are certainly a way of measuring and demonstrating our love for God and our neighbor. I've learned that in the Kingdom of God, the more you give, the more you have. I've learned that "blessed is the one who is kind to the needy" (Proverbs 14:21).

Robert Murray M'Cheyne was a pastor in Scotland, and spoke the following challenge to those in his church who did not care for the poor: *"I am concerned for the poor but more for you. I know not what Christ will say to you in the great day. I fear there are many hearing me who may know well that they are not Christians, because they do not love to give. To give largely and liberally, not grudging at all, requires a new heart; an old heart would rather part with its life-blood than its money. Oh my friends! Enjoy your money; make the most of it; give none away; enjoy it quickly for I can tell you, you will be beggars throughout eternity!"*[26]

I think that we are all generous by default. After all, we are made in the image of God and He is incredibly generous to us. I think we learn selfishness and greed as we age. But still, let me prove my point: you are a generous person. You have probably driven by a lemonade stand in your neighborhood. You saw two little girls sitting there and anticipating customers. As they stirred the lemonade, something stirred in your heart. You couldn't possibly just drive by and ignore these little girls and their desire to sell you a cup of lemonade. You pulled over the car, rolled down your window and ordered a cup. She told you the price: 50 cents. You gave her a dollar and you said three words that changed the little girl's day: "keep the change." That is generosity (or if you got your two quarters in change and drove off, we probably need to talk about your stingy heart). Of course, when you drove off, you kept your window down because you turned the corner and dumped the lemonade out. There's no way you'd drink something that she made with her filthy little hands and dirty fingernails. But in your rearview mirror, you saw her jumping up and down with joy. And you felt joy. As you get older and make money, you'll give those little girls $20 for a cup and watch them close down the lemonade stand for the rest of the day.

Author John Piper drives this point home: *"The world is not impressed when Christians get rich and say thanks to God. They are impressed when God is so satisfying that we give our riches away for Christ's sake and count it gain."*[27] The bottom line: giving is a privilege. So give generously!

CHAPTER 34

God's Economy

"God's economy is like a pie that
never runs out." — Bill Clark

M y pastor, Bill, loves pie. When we go to lunch together, he actually orders pie sometimes before he orders his meal. Pie is his love language. Even though a slice of pie makes his taste buds and stomach content, I'm convinced there's always a little disappointment when his last bite is gone. One day, he said something to me that I'll never forget: "God's economy is like a pie that never runs out."

There have been a few times in our lives when Andrea and I were at the end of our rope financially. I'd like to tell you about one specific moment in which God reminded me that He is a God of endless supply. Our international adoption fees pretty much wiped out our savings account, but when we finally got our children home from Africa, that didn't matter. We were so filled with joy that they were safely home. And then, a few weeks later, I opened an envelope that felt like Mike Tyson punching me in the stomach. Our adoption agency was asking for our remaining balance: $10,000.

$10,000 big ones.

In a single moment, I forgot about all the joy I was feeling around the homecoming of our children. I forgot about all the amazing ways God provided for us up to that point. I looked at all those zeros and internally panicked. We didn't have the money, so I started thinking of things I could sell, including my own plasma (for real). Eventually, the shock wore off and we embraced the reality printed on the bill: we owe a lot of money.

We were counting on God.

A few days later, I got a phone call from a nice lady with the Guidestone Investment Management Department. One month earlier, we had moved to a new city and joined the staff at a new church. She was calling to ask me what I wanted to do with my account. You know what I asked...

"What account?"

She went on to tell me that in 2005, when I took my first full time ministry position, I checked a box on some form. I don't recall ever doing so. Apparently, as a 22-year-old, I agreed to have $25 taken out of my paycheck each month. She said I could transfer the account to a new one, or I could pay the penalty of cashing it out. You know what I asked next...

"After the penalty, how much would we get?"

She answered, "$9,695.29."

Coming up with $10,000.00 felt like an overwhelming task, but ten whole years before I ever laid eyes on that balance due, God took care of us. All we owed after cashing in our investment was $304.71. For more insight on this, let me compare the World's Economy to God's Economy:

The World's Economy:	God's Economy:
• Financial Independence	• Dependent on God
• Accumulation	• Subtraction
• Earthly things	• Heavenly things
• External circumstances	• Internal peace
• Self-dependent	• Holy Spirit-dependent
• Treasures that are stolen	• Treasures that are safe
• To be served	• To serve
• To acquire	• To give
• Temporary	• Eternal
• 50-Year Goals	• 10,000-Year Goals

It is easy to see that the temporary treasures on earth can be stolen or depleted. But treasures rooted in God — that's like a pie that simply doesn't run out. So which kind of treasure are you interested in?

CHAPTER 35

A Self-Assessment

*"Some people are so poor, all they
have is money." —* Bob Marley

We can all be found guilty of equating the success of our lives with the amount of money we make and what we possess. Society today works hard to convince us that happiness is rooted in financial security. John Piper says it like it is, and he certainly drops the mic with this:

> *"I will tell you what a tragedy is. I will show you how to waste your life. Consider a story from the February 1998 edition of Reader's Digest, which tells about a couple who 'took early retirement from their jobs in the Northeast five years ago when he was 59 and she was 51.' Now they live in Florida, where they cruise on their 30-foot trawler, play softball and collect shells. At first, when I read it I thought it might be a joke. A spoof on the American Dream. But it wasn't.*
>
> *Tragically, this was the dream: Come to the end of your life—your one and only precious, God-given life—and let the last great work of your life, before you give an account to your Creator, be this: playing softball and collecting shells.*

> *Picture them before Christ at the great Day of Judgment: 'Look, Lord. See my shells.' That is a tragedy. And people today are spending billions of dollars to persuade you to embrace that tragic dream. Over against that, I put my protest: Don't buy it. Don't waste your life.*"[28]

If your heart is beating, you'll inevitably feel persuaded every once in a while to chase the tragic dream mentioned above. Therefore, let me offer a few challenges that can help you live a little differently when it comes to your financial prosperity:

1. Waste less on yourself and give more to others.
2. Survey what you have and put it to good use.
3. Conduct a self-evaluation to determine where you find your contentment. Have an honest conversation within. Are you on your way to discovering the secret of being content (Philippians 4:12)? If not, what needs to change?

PART FIVE
SEX

Because of the way young boys aggressively pursue sex these days, I have adopted an application written for any boy that is interested in dating one of my daughters. The application will include questions like:

- Do you own a van, a truck with oversized tires, or a waterbed?
- When is a good time to interview your parents and your pastor?
- What do you want to be if you grow up?
- If you were beaten, what is the last bone you'd hope to be broken?
- In 50 words or less, what does "don't touch my daughter" mean to you?

The closing statement on the contract will read: *"Thank you for your interest. Please allow 4-6 years for processing. You will be contacted in writing if you are approved. Please do not try to contact me in any way. If your application is rejected, you will be notified by two gentlemen wearing white ties and carrying violin cases."*

But, seriously.

In college, "dating" can be interpreted in countless different ways. There is a story of a dean addressing college freshmen on their first day on campus. "Here are the rules," he said. "The female dormitory will be off limits for all male students, and the male dormitory will be off limits for all female students. Anybody caught breaking this rule will be fined $20. If you are caught breaking this rule a second time, you will be fined $60. The third time you are caught, you will be fined $180. Are there any questions?"

A young man stood up and asked, *"How much for a season pass?"*

As a college pastor, I saw it all. I saw students who had never dated anyone and were still waiting on their first kiss. I saw students who had dated, but not compromised their boundaries. Some students refrained from having sex, but willingly crossed every other line. I met college students who were virgins, but consistently struggled with pornography, masturbation, or lust. I met many students who were still in the process of healing from sexual assault, sexual abuse, or rape. I met students who were exploring their sexuality by pursuing same-sex relationships, and others who were proudly and openly gay. I met students who were filled with regret for losing their virginity, and others who proudly kept count of how many people they had slept with. I had students in my ministry who got pregnant and graciously gave the baby up for adoption, and others who regrettably had an abortion. I had students who were confused with their own gender. Again, I saw it all and nothing really surprised me. Whatever your current situation is, let's explore sexuality a bit.

CHAPTER 36

Sexual Attraction

"Wow... what do we do with this?"
— Adam and Eve (probably)

God created man and woman, *from head to toe*. That means, friends, that God created the male's penis and the female's vagina. Every bit of your anatomy was God's idea. And how it works was God's idea, too. Awkward? Not at all.

In the opening pages of Scripture, we learn that God created everything and He referred to everything as "good." Except that one thing that wasn't good: Adam was alone. So God created Eve (thank you, Lord!). Let's consider how this scene unfolded, at least in my own mind.

> Adam and Eve were enjoying life in the most beautiful garden in history — like Yellowstone National Park on steroids. They drank water from the streams, ate delicious fruits and vegetables, listened to birds sing, and cuddled with little animals. Their senses were constantly stimulated by hundreds of sights, smells, sounds, and tastes. I imagine every day they discovered something new, such as a new species of butterfly, a never before seen flower, or a hummingbird. Everything was

pleasant, including the weather. The temperatures were so enjoyable that they lived in the nude!

While life was all good, it was about to get unimaginably better. Kind of like Christmas morning, after you've opened all of your presents and your dad says, "wait a minute, I think there's one more!" Then, he walks to the closet to pull out the biggest box you've ever seen. *The grand finale.* In the same way, God said to Adam and Eve one day: "Multiply and fill the earth." Think about Adam and Eve's dinner conversation that night. They were outside having their usual picnic dinner under the stars, trying to figure out what it means to multiply. *How do we multiply?* The Bible doesn't say that God gave the couple a sex manual.

They had to figure out this stuff on their own!

Once God awakened arousal in man and woman, their evening picnic took an extravagant detour. Sitting there naked, as usual, Adam looked at Eve differently. He watched her lips bite into a strawberry, and then his eyes lowered, studying each and every curvature of her body. In that moment, sexual attraction became a thing.

Eve then said to him, *"Adam, what is that? What do we do with that?"* I don't know how long it took them to figure it out, but I assure you, they did.

That night in the Garden of Eden ended with a grand finale (the very first God-honoring orgasm...maybe two). I illustrate that story for one purpose: to remind you that sex all originated as a gift from God. Consider the alternatives: He created the queen bee to mate once in her life. He created some species that reproduce without a mate (*parthenogenesis reproduction*). He created species like the clouded leopard that only mate every December. And the poor praying mantis…after the male flaps his wings and sways his abdomen to get a female's attention, they get it on. Immediately following intercourse, she thanks him by decapitating him. While that sounds awful, I guess it's the best way to go.

Then, there's mankind. We are invited to enjoy sex, as often as we want, however we want, and with whomever we want, but — *wait* — within the context of God's design. That is: one man and one woman sharing in a faithful, monogamous, heterosexual marriage covenant that embodies the virtue of sacrificial love that we find in Jesus.

CHAPTER 37

Why Sex?

"Be fruitful and multiply." — God

If you have had sex, are currently sexually active, or crossing your fingers that someone will have sex with you in college, have you asked yourself *why?* I can think of a few motivations or reasons that might apply to you:

- Impatience (waiting for marriage may seem impossible)
- Pleasure (duh, it feels awesome)
- Curiosity (basic anatomy)
- Intoxication (drunk people sleep with just about anyone)
- Rebellion (for your entire life, your parents and your youth pastor told you not to have sex, and you're done with their advice)
- Boredom (it's the weekend...what else is there to do?)
- Acceptance (you simply refuse to be the only virgin in your group of peers, or some loser convinced you that you have to have sex to be worthy of a relationship)
- Freedom (enjoy sex now while you're young and single!)
- Love (there's nothing wrong with it if we're getting married, right?)

While there are a variety of reasons that people explore sexuality, I propose to you that God created sex to procreate. But thankfully, there's more. The sperm and the egg definitely share the responsibility to populate the earth, but we aren't clouded leopards who only get lucky every December. Husbands and wives are given sex for visual, physical and emotional satisfaction as often as they want! Sex within marriage is an expression of mutual love and submission, and trust me, it is *not boring* just because you're hitched. Sex with your spouse should actually improve over time, as you've had more time to study one another and learn new tricks. Proverbs 5:18-19 beautifully dismantles any speculation that sex with your spouse will be lame. Check it out:

> *May your fountain be blessed, and may you rejoice in the wife of your youth. A loving doe, a graceful deer — may her breasts satisfy you always, may you ever be intoxicated by her love.* (Proverbs 5:18-19)

Come on. This is too good to be true. Sisters, you deserve a husband who will rejoice in you, not an immature, horny college kid that wants no-strings-attached sex. You deserve a husband that is captivated by you, not a dude that only sees your legs. You deserve a *man* who will pursue you for marriage — not a *boy* who only pursues you to take you to bed. You are invited to be a loving doe and a graceful deer to your husband, which is a tender, pleasant, innocent companion. You deserve a husband who will be satisfied with you always, which means he won't choose to seek pleasure elsewhere (he won't have an affair with one of his co-workers or thousands of affairs with images online). There's a man out there that will be intoxicated by your love — choose him over the fraternity guy who's intoxicated on cheap beer and desperately inviting you to his dorm room.

While the Bible gives plenty of warnings and instructions on how to protect love, Proverbs 5:18-19 clearly reveals seven amazing possibilities that await you in marriage:

1. Blessing (may your fountain be blessed)
2. Delight (rejoice in the wife of your youth)
3. Companionship (a loving doe, a graceful deer)
4. Pleasure (may her breasts satisfy you)
5. Faithfulness ("always" and "ever be")
6. Satisfaction (intoxicated with love)
7. Love (mutual feelings not based on pleasure alone)

I hate to rain on your parade, but having sex with the first five people you meet in college is not going to result in blessing, delight, companionship, pleasure, faithfulness, satisfaction and love. Ok, maybe pleasure. But the fleeting, surface-level, dangerous, careless, regretful, meaningless kind of pleasure. I hope I have you thinking at this point that your sexuality should be protected and cherished.

CHAPTER 38

Sex in the Bible

"Awake, north wind, and come, south wind!
Blow on my garden, that its fragrance may
spread everywhere. Let my beloved come
into his garden and taste its choice fruits."
— The Beloved, Song of Solomon 4:16

There are many sexual encounters mentioned in the Bible that are not God-honoring. I'll avoid the details, but some people in history did some really twisted stuff. However, there is one particular story that describes what God desires for all of us: a profoundly meaningful, satisfying sexual relationship between a *husband and his wife.*

Many young people who are unfamiliar with the Bible are oblivious to the fact that God is very interested in human sexuality! He is not some boring, prude, white-bearded grandpa in the sky, pointing His finger at you, threatening you to keep your pants on. He created erotic pleasure and intimacy! He is the brain behind the brilliance of sex! But it is only brilliant in the context for which He created it.

In Song of Solomon, intimacy between a man and his wife is illustrated with the most exciting and intriguing terms (I'll leave it up to your imagination to determine what these terms represent): *Apples, clusters, garden, entering the garden, fruit, dew, gazelle, lilies, lovesick, mountains, stag, palm tree, vine, vineyard, and pleasant fruits.* In the text, we not only see intimacy and excitement, but also the void of shame and guilt. They didn't wake up wondering, *"why did we do that?"* or *"what was his name again?"* Instead, they experienced the joy and thrill of God's gift of sexual intimacy. You can go read the scene on your own.

Simply put, it is awesome God's way, and it is better His way, too.

As a young, unmarried person, God isn't saying, "no, sex is bad!" Instead, He is saying, "yes, sex is wonderful, but wait." So, let's talk about waiting.

CHAPTER 39

Purity

"Nothing has stolen more dreams, dashed more hopes, broken up more families, and messed up more people psychologically than our propensity to disregard God's commands regarding sexual purity." — Andy Stanley

When you read Song of Solomon, you quickly realize that it was God's idea for sex to be out of this world. Sex is also remarkably sacred. God's interest in your sexuality is so much more than merely asking you to "behave" until you're married. Again, God created you to be a sexual being. But He wants you to experience it in the best form and fashion: marriage.

I love how Eugene Peterson translates the words of Paul written in 1 Corinthians. This is from his Message Version of the Bible:

> There's more to sex than mere skin on skin. Sex is as much spiritual mystery as physical fact. As written in Scripture, "The two become one." Since we want to become spiritually one with the Master, we must not pursue the kind of sex that avoids commitment and intimacy, leaving us more lonely than ever—the kind of sex that can never "become one." There is a sense

in which sexual sins are different from all others. In sexual sin we violate the sacredness of our own bodies, these bodies that were made for God-given and God-modeled love, for "becoming one" with another. Or didn't you realize that your body is a sacred place, the place of the Holy Spirit? Don't you see that you can't live however you please, squandering what God paid such a high price for? The physical part of you is not some piece of property belonging to the spiritual part of you. God owns the whole works. So let people see God in and through your body.[29]

In sexual sin, we violate the sacredness of our own bodies. So purity is refusing to compromise something sacred, and instead, choosing to protect God's unique purpose for your mind and body. Authors Eric and Leslie Ludy define purity as "the flexing of a moral muscle within a human soul, a moment-by-moment choice to walk a path of integrity amid a world polluted with sin. Innocence is a state of being, but purity is a choice, a step of obedience, and a decision of the will."[30]

On a small scale, sexual impurity can feel trivial. You'll hear tons of stories of college students meeting at a party, hooking up that night, and never talking again. It's likely that you'll hear sex talked about extremely casually and sexually active people boasting about their sex life, void of any consequences. So what's the big deal? The big deal is that it is not aligned with God's original intent and purpose.

The world is guilty of corrupting sexuality; perverting the very gift that originated in the Garden of Eden, where man and woman become one flesh. Statistics show that young people are experimenting sexually more than ever before, and the "one flesh" moment in many marriages comes after a long list of other fleshes that you or your spouse experienced before you two met. Sexual purity isn't just about keeping it in your pants, but it is thinking about your future. A sexual appetite is not a bad thing, but rather than satisfying your craving, accept God's invitation to wait. God asks for purity. There aren't ten or twenty or fifty shades of grey here, just black and white. We are either sexually pure, or sexually perverted.

CHAPTER 40

Perversion

*"What pornography is really about, ultimately,
isn't sex, but death."* — Susan Sontag

Perversion is to *alter something from its original course,
meaning, or state to a distortion or corruption of what
was first intended.* Specifically in this context, a pervert is a
person whose sexual behavior is regarded as abnormal and
unacceptable. While "pervert" may be a term you've called
people for saying inappropriate things in your high school
hallway, statistics reveal just how perverted our society has
become in relation to sexuality. For example:

One in four sexually active adolescent females has
an STD such as chlamydia or HPV.[31]

Every two minutes, someone is sexually
assaulted in the United States — an average of
207,754 sexual assault victims each year. Fifty-four
percent of sexual assaults are not reported to the
police, and 97% of rapists will never spend a day
in jail.[32]

Sex trafficking is the third largest international
crime industry, generating a profit of $32 billion
every year. According to the U.S. State Department,
600,000 to 800,000 people are trafficked across

international borders every year, of which 80% are female and half are children.[33]

Twelve percent of all websites are pornographic and 35% of all Internet downloads are pornographic in nature. Every second, 28,258 Internet users are viewing pornography. "Sex" is the most searched word on the Internet and 70% of Internet porn traffic occurs during the 9am-5pm workday.[34]

Infidelity has been found as the single most cited cause of divorce in over 150 cultures.[35]

These statistics are overwhelmingly disheartening, I know. It proves, though, that humanity is guilty of perverting sexuality and it is unhealthy and destructive in every way imaginable. Let me address an issue that is one of the most prevalent in today's world: pornography.

Pornography trains you to practice lust and live in a fantasy world of evil thoughts. The more you burn with lust, the more desperate you become for gratification. When I was a child, pornography was a stack of nudity magazines with women provocatively posing for a photo. No one could ever access the "good stuff" as it was only found online, and you needed a credit card. My generation was taught not to look at porn, because we had a choice (or in my case, no access). Your generation needs to be told what to do *when you see it*, because inevitably, you'll see it (if you don't already look at it multiple times a day). Here's what you should do when you see it: run like Usain Bolt on speed. Friend, it will destroy you.

FOR YOUNG MEN: Many college students think, "I'll stop looking at porn when I get married." I'm here to tell you, you won't. Porn destroys families and eliminates trust. It totally distorts and perverts your expectations of sex in marriage. On too many occasions, I have met with a young man who has watched so much pornography that it has a negative impact on his intimacy with his wife. Oh, how God must grieve when a man can't enjoy the wife of his youth because of the thousands of images of airbrushed, artificial women archived in his mind. Even worse, almost 90% of pornographic scenes include physical aggression toward the woman.[36] Fellas, someday, you might have the privilege of tender lovemaking with your wife. In case you lack common sense, let me inform you — she won't want to be slapped and choked like you've maybe seen in porn scenes. Pornography dehumanizes women, making them appear as an object rather than a daughter of God and your sister in Christ. If you are currently hooked on pornography, I hope this helps to wake you up. If you think you will marry a woman one day who will let you recreate all of your favorite scenes from over the years, that is foolishness. Put an end to this now. Get help.[37]

CHAPTER 41

Late Night Texts

"You up?" — 2:15am Text Message

I implore you: don't say "yes" to the idiot texting you after midnight soliciting a cheap, meaningless hook up. That person doesn't have the desire or the maturity to pursue you or marry you, and he or she is likely texting and sleeping with multiple other people throughout the week. You're just another stop on their tour to physical gratification, and you might even need to wear a nametag to help eliminate confusion.

"Thanks, Sarah. When can we do this again?"

"It's Stephanie. Get your things and get out."

And as he leaves, you're left wondering if you were his first or second or third text that night. Most of the time, the casual, friends-with-benefits, "this is the last time we're going to do this" encounters are sponsored by selfishness, booze, and regret. To be super blunt — if you are the one receiving the text, you are being used. You are better than that! The more you think about it, the more it makes sense to ignore the text and go back to bed, alone. The next morning, you won't be sleepy. And you won't be sorry, either.

CHAPTER 42

Dumb Oxen

"Come to bed with me." — Potiphar's Wife

This chapter is for young men.

In Genesis 39, we read part of the story of a man named Joseph. This guy worked for Potiphar, the commander of the royal guard in Pharaoh's court. Potiphar trusted Joseph so much that he put him in charge of everything he owned. The only problem was that Potiphar traveled for work, and in his absence, his naughty wife couldn't take her eyes off of Joseph.

"Come to bed with me," she suggested (Genesis 39:7). Joseph could have taken any one of her invitations and had outstanding, no-strings-attached sex with Mrs. Potiphar. Instead, he responded:

> *"No one is greater in this house than I am. My master has withheld nothing from me except you, because you are his wife. How then could I do such a wicked thing and sin against God?" And though she spoke to Joseph day after day, he refused to go to bed with her or even be with her. One day he went into the house to attend to his duties, and none of the household servants were inside. She caught him by his cloak and said, "Come to bed with me!" But he left his cloak in her hand and ran out of the house. (Genesis 39:9-10)*

Either Potiphar was lame in bed, or Joseph looked like Channing Tatum. Regardless, he was persistently seduced by another man's wife. Here's some perspective for you: any young lady you meet in college that entices you and invites you to have sex with her is also another man's wife. Learn from Joseph's example and run. Run like Forrest Gump — just keep running and running and running.

Not every man in the Bible demonstrated such self-control when faced with the temptation or opportunity to have sex. The Hall of Faith in the Bible teaches us that sex has the power to destroy a man, no matter how strong or spiritual or wise he may be.

Sampson was the judge over Israel. He was given extraordinary strength and killed a lion with his hands. Who do you know that has killed a lion with his hands? No one. He murdered over 1,000 people with the jawbone of a donkey. But a woman, Delilah, misled and deceived him. She seduced him and he lost his strength, and eventually his life. David was a king and great military leader. He was loved and well respected. He saw a naked neighbor bathing and summoned her to have sex with him. He got her pregnant and had her husband murdered on the battlefield in order to sweep his mistake under the rug. His story will be elaborated on in chapter 49. Solomon was (and still is) the wisest man to ever live. Even with his matchless wisdom, he was so sexually infatuated with foreign women, he was eventually introduced to false gods. Eventually, his theology was polluted and he compromised his faithfulness to the one true God.

Extraordinarily strong, devoted, and wise men can still fall to the seductress woman. Luckily, the Bible offers clear warning signs of a girl that is up to no good:

1. Her lips are as pleasing to the carnal senses of men as honey is sweet to the taste (Proverbs 5:3).
2. Her speech is enticing and flattering, and her seductive expressions prey upon your heart with the intention of you yielding to her temptations (Proverbs 7:21).
3. She's not interested in commitment and depends on her appearance to determine your actions (Proverbs 7:10-12).

The results of yielding to the seduction of a woman are not in your favor. If her lips, complimentary words, indecent clothing, and promiscuous behavior put you in a trance, you might enjoy the next 4-5 minutes with her. But, she's given you more than her body. She's given you a death sentence:

o You're led to death; to the grave (Proverbs 5:4)
o You're unhappy in old age (Proverbs 5:11)
o You're ensnared, held down and led astray (Proverbs 5:22-23)
o You're reduced to a loaf of bread (Proverbs 6:26)
o You're punished (Proverbs 6:29)
o You're destroyed (Proverbs 6:32)
o You're like an ox going to your slaughter (Proverbs 7:22)
o You're like a deer stepping into a noose (Proverbs 7:23)
o You're like a bird darting into a snare (Proverbs 7:23)

Young brother, don't be a dumb ox. Run from women like Potiphar's wife. Run from the tempting Bathsheba. Run from the seductress Delilah. Run until your chest hurts and you have that nagging pain in your side. Just keep running and running and running.

CHAPTER 43

Pig with a Nose Ring

"Modesty isn't about covering up our bodies because they're bad. Modesty isn't about hiding ourselves…it's about revealing our dignity." — Jessica Rey

This chapter is for young women.

I'm not into fashion at all. However, I do believe many young women today own wardrobes that are meant to be worn at a gym, not in class or at church. Proverbs 11:22 says, "Like a gold ring in a pig's snout is a beautiful woman without discretion." I mean no disrespect, ladies, as you are obviously the more attractive gender on planet Earth. But there is something to learn about the farm animal mentioned by Solomon in this verse. To lack discretion could mean:

- Dressing lustfully to flaunt your image
- Speaking shamelessly with young men
- Purposefully pursuing sexual promiscuity
- Willingly allowing a man to use your body as a playground

- Intentionally posting half-naked images of yourself on social media
- Deliberately teasing young men with sexual suggestions

I believe Proverbs 11:22 is calling you to walk through your college years with forethought. Zoom out of the weeds and look at the big picture. Should I really be dating this guy? Do I really need to jump party to party? Is this healthy or wise to give my body to others so freely? Is this behavior beneficial in the long run? Asking yourself questions like these can save you from internal and external danger.

Instead, dear sister, "Charm is deceitful, and beauty is fleeting; but a woman who fears the LORD is to be praised." (Proverbs 31:30) Why is beauty fleeting? Because you're aging. Sure, this very moment you are not concerned with the physical ramifications of getting older, but in a decade or two, you'll notice a wrinkle between your eyebrows that will drive you crazy. You may still be carrying weight you gained during pregnancy. Breastfeeding changes the look of things. In many other ways, gravity will win (just ask your grandmother).

Therefore, be prayerful and cautious about the men that pursue you in college. If they don't submit the idea of pursuing you in a God-honoring fashion, tell them to get lost. Settle down with a man who defines your beauty not only by what you look like, but by who you are.

CHAPTER 44

STDs

"We have reached a decisive moment for the nation. STD rates are rising, and many of the country's systems for preventing STDs have eroded." — Dr. Jonathan Mermin

When you hear "STD," a couple things come to mind. First, your 6th grade school counselor who hit play on the most awkward DVD you've ever seen. Second, "that won't happen to me, I'll use a condom." Ok, its true — the 6th grade sexual education video was, indeed, awkward. But, my friend, condoms can't be trusted to fully protect you.

Medical doctor and author Meg Meeker shares some alarming statistics from her research on sexually transmitted diseases:

- One in five Americans over age twelve tests positive for genital herpes.
- Herpes type 2 infections increased 500% during the 1980s.
- There are 5-6 million new cases of HPV infections annually.
- HPV is spread through sexual contact. Some HPV strains cause cancer, some don't. HPV is responsible

for approximately 99% of all cervical cancer cases in women.

- A teen girl is at greater risk for dangerous sexually transmitted diseases because the skin overlying her cervix is immature.
- As many as 90% of people infected with herpes type 2 don't know they are infected.[38]

Hopefully human papillomavirus infection, genital herpes, chlamydia, gonorrhea, AIDS, and syphilis are words that you never hear a medical professional say after one of your annual exams. I've sat with many students as they opened results from a doctor to learn whether or not their previous partner had given them one of those nasty, unwanted gifts. I sat with one young man who held an envelope in his hand revealing results from his HIV test. He handed it to me and said, "Open it, please." As I started to, he ran around the corner and threw up before I could even tell him his test was negative. The anxiety alone made him physically sick.

Beyond the initial shock of the diagnosis, there are a variety of medical complications and consequences that can result from an STD: infertility, pelvic inflammatory disease, chronic pelvic pain, tubal pregnancies, urethral infection, swollen testicles, vaginal discharge, painful urination, fever, fatigue, ulcers, headaches, rashes, mental illness, blindness, and even death.

I promise you, your odds are much better if you abstain from sexual activity.

CHAPTER 45

Safe Sex

"Condoms aren't completely safe.
My friend was wearing one and he
got hit by a bus." — Bob Rubin

The safest sex is when you're wearing a wedding ring, not a condom. However, 85% of people who use condoms as their birth control method effectively prevent pregnancy.[39] That seems like a high percentage and the odds are in your favor, until you're one of the 15/100 who pee on a pregnancy test and tell your partner you're expecting a child, and that "safe sex" wasn't so safe after all.

Condoms are notoriously marketed as "Extra Thin" or "Bare Skin" in order to promote protected sex that almost feels like the "real thing." Yet, there are countless jokes claiming that protected sex feels like showering in a plastic jumpsuit, or getting a back massage while wearing a North Face jacket. Even the super thin rubbers aren't all they're made out to be. The "real thing" is within the context in which God desires for you.

Just a word of caution for any young women considering oral contraceptives: If a girl takes oral contraceptives for more than five years, she is four times more likely to develop cervical cancer.[40] No matter how you might be preparing to enjoy consequence-free sex in college, you are not fire proof. Instead, imagine a sex life in which you aren't constantly worried about pregnancy, gonorrhea and chlamydia, a tarnished reputation, or regret the next morning. That kind of sex life is with your spouse!

CHAPTER 46

How Far is Too Far?

"Wanna come watch Netflix and chill?" — The Desperate

When I was young, sexual activity was described through the analogy of a baseball diamond. Of course, first base was getting a kiss and home plate was "going all the way." Really – that was the terminology a few decades ago. "Did you go all the way?" Times have changed and first base isn't so innocent anymore. What hasn't changed is the ambiguity of what it means to "hook up." While many people consider "hooking up" as intercourse, other people will sit on the couch, kiss a while, and then brag to their roommates that they "hooked up" with someone. To make matters more complicated, the baseball analogy has lost its appeal, as there are more modern illustrations of getting some action. For example, if someone asks you to "come watch Netflix and chill," they're not inviting you over for popcorn and a movie, but instead, crossing their fingers for a home run.

Centuries ago, there was no concept of dating. Yes, people still had sex outside of marriage, but it was more frowned upon and taboo. Historically, dating and intercourse were reserved for after marriage, as many cultures arranged marriage for you. Therefore, dating for three years and being engaged for another year while burning with sexual passion for one another is a relatively newer idea for relationships. Paul wrote to this problem in the Bible: if you can't control yourself, you should marry, as it's better to go to the chapel and get married than burn with passion and lust. (1 Corinthians 7:9) Throughout history, young people had three basic choices:

1. Remain single and abstinent.
2. Live immorally and have sex with multiple partners.
3. Get married.

What our culture promotes is #2 with a twist: since you don't want to be single, and you're too young or broke to be married, have sex with multiple partners and don't worry about the morality issue.

So, how far is too far? 1 Corinthians 6:18 says to "flee from sexual immorality." We're back to that Forrest Gump thing again. To flee is to run, like Joseph did. From the Bible, we see that kissing results in plenty of arousal: "Your lips drop sweetness as honeycomb, my bride, milk and honey are on your tongue." (Song of Solomon 4:11) Also, "His lips are like lilies, dripping with myrrh." (Song of Solomon 5:13) I can confidently conclude that kissing is foreplay. I encourage you to stop at kissing, and stay in control when kissing. Stay vertical and out of each other's bedrooms. If you're tempted, meet up for coffee in public. The chances of you rounding second or third base in Starbucks are pretty thin.

CHAPTER 47

Missionary Dating

"Don't let your loneliness turn into stupid." — Justin Graves

I met with many students who had a physical attraction and an emotional connection with someone of a different religious affiliation. If you are a Christian, there are boundaries here you would be wise to follow. Second Corinthians 6:14 says, "Do not be yoked together with unbelievers. For what do righteousness and wickedness have in common? Or what fellowship can light have with darkness?"

A yoke is a crosspiece device that joins a pair of matching animals together for work, like oxen. Being yoked together is the idea of mutual fellowship, harmony, agreement, and shared values. Have you ever seen an ox and a goat working well together, pulling the same weight? No. It simply doesn't work!

I've heard this called "Missionary Dating," which is when a Christian person dates a non-Christian person with hopes of converting that person to Christianity. Mark my words: this is a recipe for disaster. More often than not, "Missionary Dating" will result in the missionary position. Don't date someone with the expectation that he or she will change for you. Date someone for who he or she already is, and then change, learn and grow together.

CHAPTER 48

Your Future Spouse

"Your sexual past doesn't have to haunt you." — Brittany Ann

Author Leslie Ludy shares a realization she had when reading Proverbs 31. She read to honor her husband "all the days of her life." Prior to meeting him, she asked herself, "What if my future husband could see me interacting with the opposite sex *now?* Would he feel honored and loved by what I'm doing?"[41] That is definitely a question worth asking yourself as you begin to interact romantically with others during college.

I had a college student one time meet me for coffee. He told me he had too much to drink the weekend before and woke up the next morning with a young woman in his bed. Not only did he not remember if they had "protected sex," but he also didn't know the name of the young woman in his bed.

I could tell his initial concern was whether or not they used condom. He was scared and asked, *"How could I get so drunk that I'd risk getting a girl pregnant or getting an STD?"* I took the conversation down a different path — I cared a lot more about that precious young woman than I did his fear of genital warts. I said something to him like, *"Somewhere right now, your future wife is waking up. Would it bother you right now if she had a young man in her bed who didn't know her name? Think of how you treated that young woman last night. Would it bother you if someone treated your future bride and mother of your children the same way?"*

I thought he was going to throw up his latte.

If for no other reason, don't sleep around in college out of respect for your future spouse. Don't settle for cheap, dirty, and meaningless intimacy. Save it for your honeymoon. There's a strong chance you and your future fiancé will have a conversation about your sexual past. I hope it is a conversation that you can have looking him or her in the eye.

CHAPTER 49

Sexual Abuse

"We must send a message across the world that there is no disgrace in being a survivor of sexual violence — the shame is on the aggressor." — Angelina Jolie

King David is a hero in ancient history, and especially for young men. Why? Because he was "a man after God's own heart." (1 Samuel 13:14) Yet, even in the midst of his great impact on the history of the nation of Israel, his sexual appetite resulted in a modern day crime that would have left the king behind bars for rape and murder.

To summarize what happened (as documented in 2 Samuel 11): King David sent his men to battle, but decided to stay in Jerusalem. One late afternoon, when he woke up from his nap, he was strolling around the roof of the palace. There in the distance, he saw a stunningly beautiful woman bathing on the rooftop. David sent his men to find out about her — she was Bathsheba, wife of Uriah *(one of David's most honored and trusted soldiers)* and granddaughter of one of David's most trusted advisors. David knew Uriah was at battle, so he had Bathsheba brought to his palace, and his bed.

In 2 Samuel 11:4, the Hebrew word describing what happened to Bathsheba is *"laqach"* (pronounced law-kakh').

She was *taken* to David, and I'm sure it wasn't long after her arrival to the palace that the King of Israel forced himself upon her. The Bible didn't mention that she resisted or ran, which doesn't convince me that she joyfully skipped to the palace, excited for a chance to roll around in royal bed sheets. She did what she was told, as it was not wise to refuse royalty.

A horrifying amount of women will experience forced intercourse in their lifetime. To be clear, a woman doesn't become a victim solely after penetration. The following definitions might be helpful:

Rape is a type of sexual assault involving sexual intercourse or other forms of sexual penetration carried out against a person without that person's consent. *Sexual Assault* is sexual contact that involves force upon a person without consent or is inflicted upon a person who is incapable of giving consent (due to age or physical/mental incapacity). *Sexual Harassment* involves unwanted sexual advances or obscene, vulgar remarks. All three are incredibly wrong and all three are present on your college campus. People are victims of all three each and every day.

Victims of sexual assault have been known to wait to speak out; particularly female victims. This is incredibly true in our culture today, as women are speaking out on sexual assault instances that occurred up to 30 or 40 years ago. Writer Sara Miller offers a few reasons for the delay in accusations, none of which are more important than you feeling physically safe and emotionally secure:

- Society tends to blame the woman, as the charges ruin the man's life.
- A cultural belief that "good women don't get raped."

- Feelings of personal responsibility or blame for the assault.
- Speaking out can be very painful and cause personal embarrassment.
- Fear of accusing a high-power individual or social figure.[42]

If you have been a victim of sexual assault, let me sensitively counsel you to get help. The kind of help you should pursue is for you to determine. You may find resolve by talking to your roommate, your parent, a pastor, or a therapist. You may find healing and move on, or you might call the local police and file a restraining order or press charges. There will be a process of emotional healing that could take weeks or decades. Again, it is not my place to tell you exactly how to respond to what's happened to you... I simply want to encourage you not to walk through this alone. There is no shame whatsoever — the shame is on the aggressor.

For your safety and further education, I want to offer a few *misconceptions* about sexual assault. Again, these come from author Sara Miller:

1. Sexual assault is usually committed by strangers. (According to the Rape, Abuse and Incest National Network, less than 25% of sexual assault cases are committed by strangers. Rather, 43% of sexual assaults are committed by friends or acquaintances.)
2. Sexual assault is provoked by the victim's actions. (Victims don't provoke sexual assault, but "victim blaming" is very common. While an assault is a choice made by a perpetrator, many will blame the victim, claiming they were "asking for it.")

3. If the victim doesn't struggle against the perpetrator, it's not assault. (Many victims freeze or feel obligated to comply. Furthermore, they may not fight if they are aware of their physical inferiority.)[43]

While this chapter has offered definitions and misconceptions about sexual assault, Chapter 54 (Date Rape) will specifically address any young men who would dare to drug a young woman in order to satisfy his sexual desires. Such an act is one that only the scum of the Earth would commit.

CHAPTER 50

Abortion

"I've noticed that everyone who is for abortion has already been born." — Ronald Reagan

O dds are, someone will read this book that has had an abortion. To you, I say: you are precious in God's sight. You are beautifully and wonderfully made. God's grace is sufficient for you. This chapter is not intended in any way to cast guilt or blame your direction, and if continuing to read is too painful, please feel the liberty to turn to Chapter 51.

> [13] For you created my inmost being; you knit me together in my mother's womb. [14] I praise you because I am fearfully and wonderfully made; your works are wonderful, I know that full well. [15] My frame was not hidden from you when I was made in the secret place, when I was woven together in the depths of the earth. [16] Your eyes saw my unformed body; all the days ordained for me were written in your book before one of them came to be.
> — Psalm 139:13-16

Knit together. Wonderfully made. Intricately woven.
Scientifically, at the moment of conception (when a man's sperm and a woman's egg tango), there is a new life

possessing 46 chromosomes that are completely distinct from the mother and the father. Genetically speaking, at the moment of conception, an embryo has a completely different genetic code than both the mother and father. Most abortions occur just past 8 weeks, when the fetus is sucking her thumb. She's responding to sounds and her organs are developing. Her brain is functioning. Her heart is pumping. Her liver is making blood cells. Her kidneys are cleaning fluid. She has fingerprints. For crying out loud, we are identified by our fingerprints! How does an unborn child with fingerprints ever get classified as not having an identity? Many pro-choice people would never refer to this as a "baby," but a "product of conception." Ok, but the "product" has a beating heart and is sucking her thumb.

Want evidence of our fractured consciousness? Under Federal Law, if you disturb, mutilate or destroy a sea turtle egg, you can be punished up to $100,000 and spend a year in prison.[44] If you touch, break or steal a fertilized bald eagle egg, you can be punished up to $250,000 and be put in prison for 2 years.[45] Yet, a pregnant woman can drive to an abortion clinic and allow a doctor to legally exterminate a human child with a vacuum pump.

Here's the twist: if a pregnant woman walking to an abortion clinic is hit and killed by a car, the driver of the car would be charged with two counts of involuntary manslaughter: one for the mother and one for the child. That's right, two counts. There are laws in 38 states that recognize the unlawful killing of an unborn child as homicide, including my home state. Oklahoma's House Bill 1686 defines an "unborn child" as "the unborn offspring of human beings from the moment of conception, through pregnancy, and until live birth, including the human conceptus, zygote, morula, blastocyst, embryo, and fetus."[46]

If you experience pregnancy in college, I imagine the spike of your anxiety could lead you to consider an abortion. As the father of two adopted children, I implore you to consider delivering your child and allowing him or her the privilege of living life with an adoptive family. There are agencies that help support young pregnant women and provide services such as financial support, transportation, medical care, and housing. Additionally, you can select the adoptive family for your child, choose between open or confidential adoption, and receive counseling and emotional support.[47]

If you impregnate someone in college, you have no right to pressure her to have an abortion. You might have thoughts like: "I'm not ready to be a father," or "I can't afford this," or "what about my future?" Those are completely understandable things to panic about. But it's definitely not fair (or right) to strong-arm a young woman, pregnant with *your offspring*, to go "take care of it." She's the one lying on the table, not you. While you may truly be in no position to take financial responsibility for a child, you certainly have a choice to take responsibility of your actions and support a young woman in the decision to offer your child to an adoptive family. It is a tremendous and noble gift.

Think about it.

After you think about it, *pray about it.*

PART SIX
ALCOHOL

Surely you know the anonymous United States folk song, *"99 Bottles of Beer on the Wall..."* I find it somewhat odd that elementary kids sing this song on the school bus to kill time. When you think about it, finishing 99 beers is quite the accomplishment. But after "taking one down" and "passing it around" until the last bottle is gone, the song ends:

> *"No more bottles of beer on the wall.*
> *No more bottles of beer.*
> *Go to the store and buy some more...*
> *99 bottles of beer on the wall."*

I'm assuming after a group of friends share 99 beers, the one who goes to the store to buy some more should definitely not be driving. Simple little folk songs paint a clear picture that drinking can be casually problematic, especially in a new season of independence such as college.

Personally, I do not think drinking alcohol (at a legal age) is wrong. But, it can quickly become one. Here are a few of the warnings we see in Scripture:

- Wine is a mocker and beer a brawler; whoever is led astray by them is not wise. (Proverbs 20:1)
- Whoever loves wine will not be rich. (Proverbs 21:20)
- Be wise. Stay on the right path. Don't join those who drink too much wine. (Proverbs 23:19-20)
- Wine will bite like a snake and poisons like a viper. (Proverbs 23:32)
- He who loves pleasure will become a poor man; he who loves wine and oil will not become rich. (Proverbs 21:17)
- Do not get drunk on wine, which leads to sin. (Ephesians 5:16)

Those are biblical warnings, but if those don't grab your attention, let me offer a few warnings related to health, relationships, safety and death:

- Nearly 30% of traffic-related deaths are linked to alcohol.[48]
- More than 80,000 people die from alcohol-related deaths each year in the United States.[49]
- Alcohol poisoning kills six people every day.[50]
- Alcohol use kills 4,700 teenagers each year. That's more than all illegal drugs combined.[51]
- Women who binge drink are more likely to have unprotected sex, increasing the risk of unintended pregnancy and sexually transmitted diseases.[52]
- Binge drinking dramatically increases the risk of sexual assault on women, especially those living in a college setting.[53]
- 1,825 college students between the ages of 18 and 24 die from unintentional alcohol-related injuries each year.[54]
- 696,000 college students between the ages of 18 and 24 are assaulted by another student who has been drinking, and nearly another 100,000 report experiencing alcohol-related sexual assault or date rape.[55]
- About 1 in 4 college students report academic consequences from drinking, including missing class, falling behind in class, doing poorly on exams or papers, and receiving lower grades overall.[56]

Many new college students find it difficult to balance their social life and their academic life. However, if your social life turns into a scene in which you feel pressured to drink, be careful. Pressures can be birthed from the desire to fit in, as students might claim that drinking "like everyone else" helps them relax, have fun, meet new people, and enhance their social lives. And then there are the game day tailgate parties where students will chug beer for 3-4 hours before going in to the stadium. And then, the *post-game party*. And then sorority parties. And then...

You know what your relationship with alcohol is: either you drink, drink too much, refuse to drink, or are considering drinking. Regardless, I hope you'll pay attention to the next few chapters if you plan to drink in college.

When it comes to the worst-case scenarios, you might be thinking, *"that could never happen to me."* If you can relate to that kind of invincible mindset, let me personalize my warnings in this chapter by sharing some painful losses I have personally experienced. During college, friends of mine died from:

- Alcohol abuse
- Drunk driving
- Mixture of pills and alcohol
- Suicide (related to alcohol and drug abuse)

Over a decade later, it still feels like yesterday that I stood by their caskets and looked at their lifeless bodies. It feels like yesterday that I sat in disbelief as I watched their families grieve at the gravesites. Quite often, I think of them and the stories that could have been: marriage, family, career, and purpose. I know their purpose was not to die young in the ways that they did. And the most disappointing part to me is that each of their deaths could have been prevented. That being said, carefully read on. What I have to say could save you a lot of time, money, and dignity.

It could maybe even save your life.

CHAPTER 51

Twenty-One

"Turning 21-years-old isn't all it's cracked up to be. You have to start buying your own toilet paper." — Melanie White

You will most likely be presented the opportunity to purchase a fake ID in college, and I suggest you kindly turn it down. Here's why: it is against the law to purchase alcohol until you are 21-years-old. The law is the law, friend, and breaking the law is accompanied with serious consequences.

At one of our college ministry worship services, I cautioned students against drinking illegally and irresponsibly. When I addressed the students in the room who were not of legal age to drink, I encouraged them to bring their fake IDs to me that night. When service ended, multiple young men and women walked forward to give me their cards. I still have a few of them in my desk today as a reminder of the young people who made a smart decision that night.

I'd encourage you to do the same.

Don't get a fake ID, and if you have one, get rid of it.

Nothing good will come of it, I promise.

CHAPTER 52

Crimes

*"You can never prepare yourself enough to see
your mug shot and DUI."* — Tracey Gold

Most young drivers have driven over the speed limit and experienced the gut-wrenching feeling of the red and blue lights quickly approaching their rear bumper. What a horrible feeling! But a speeding ticket is merely a slap on the wrist compared to other offenses. Let me tell you, for the following crimes, you won't be reaching for your insurance in the glove box. Rather, you'll be reaching for the phone to call your parents from the police station. The following are offenses you definitely can't afford:

- DUI (Driving Under the Influence) or DWI (Driving While Intoxicated): if you're under the influence of alcohol, you are not capable of reacting quickly or efficiently, resulting in horrible and often deadly decisions. Penalties are generally the most severe of any intoxication crime and can lead to serious professional, financial, and personal difficulties, including jail time. That's not a fun phone call to make to your parents.
- Public Intoxication: when you drink so much that you're loud, aggressive, belligerent, and disruptive, you

begin disturbing others and putting them in danger. Most jurisdictions simply enforce this crime to remove obnoxious drunks from public places and isolate them in a jail cell until they sober up. That's not a fun phone call to make to your parents, either.

- Open Container: the crime that's been identified to prevent public intoxication.

- MIP (Minor in Possession): the most common offense on university campuses, as approximately half of all students are illegally consuming alcohol under the age of twenty-one.[57]

I have a dear friend who told me about his heavy drinking habits in college. He was the life of the party. While he got behind the wheel countless times completely intoxicated, he made it home every time. His flirting with danger carried into adulthood, and driving home drunk one evening, he survived an incredibly violent car wreck. Thank God, there were no other vehicles involved.

If this happens in college, and you were lucky enough to live through the accident, your parents would be buried in a pile of hospital bills and attorney fees. But when it happens in adulthood, as it did my friend, you have to explain to your spouse and children what happened. While his family was forgiving, he still made the wise decision to never drive a car again after a drink.

You can learn the easy way or the hard way. The choice is yours.

CHAPTER 53

Drunk Driving

"A tree never hits an automobile, except in self-defense." — Woody Allen

Every two minutes, someone is injured in a drunk driving crash.[58] Not everyone goes home with stiches or casts, though. In 2017, 10,874 people were killed in crashes involving a drunk driver.[59] As in, *dead*, and no longer with us. Well, the irresponsible drivers get killed, but the innocent elderly lady driving home from visiting her grandchildren, or the father of three driving home late from a work meeting — those people aren't killed by drunk drivers. They're *murdered*. See, we think of murder as the senseless use of guns and knives. But, the college dude who slams beers all night with his buddies and decides to drive home — his weapon is a 4,000-pound machine made of aluminum, steel, and rubber.

I know the gut-wrenching story of one young college student. She was out with her friends and used her fake ID to purchase drinks. Vodka tonic, followed by a Long Island Iced Tea, followed by vodka and 7-Up. Then, a shot of Jagermeister. She recalls feeling tipsy, but *not drunk*. Later that night, she thought she was ok to drive. She climbed behind the wheel and five of her friends jumped in for a ride home. Moments later, her car was wrapped around a tree. She had internal

Let's Be Honest Are You Really Ready for College?

bleeding, a lacerated liver and spleen, a punctured colon, multiple injuries from shattered glass, and four fractures in her back. The next morning, she woke up in the ICU, hooked up to countless machines and monitors. Eventually, when they slowly pulled her off of pain medication, her memory started to return and her loved ones broke the news to her: three of her friends were dead.

She was out having fun with her friends.

She felt ok to drive.

And then she went to prison. And worse, three people died.

There is certainly no excuse for driving drunk, as countless driving services are accessible and affordable from an app on your phone. To drive under the influence of alcohol is one of the most selfish, potentially costly decisions you could ever make in your life, as it could take your life, and potentially the life of others.

CHAPTER 54

Date Rape

"Young men need to be socialized in a way that rape is as unthinkable to them as cannibalism." — Mary Pipher

A date rape drug is a drug that causes temporary loss of memory or inhibition, secretly given to someone in order to facilitate rape or sexual abuse. This drug will not be far from you during college, so in this chapter, let me speak to three individuals: the potential victim, the bystander, and the offender.

To the potential victim: if you are ever in a social setting in which people are drinking alcohol, you must know that you are at risk, even if everyone at the party is a friend, or a friend of a friend. I assure you, there are people at parties that care a lot more about using you for their sexual gratification than becoming your friend. Date rape drugs weaken a victim so they are unable to resist or fight back when threatened. Worse, they weaken a victim's inhibitions, meaning he or she will become partially or fully unconscious. The very best way to avoid becoming a victim is to refuse any beverages offered to you by anyone you don't know and trust. If you choose to drink socially, prepare your own beverages. Beer cans are the safest beverages, as they can be individually opened. Community bottles of wine or liquor aren't safe. If you are ever in a setting in which you have unexplained changes in your consciousness, immediately share with a trusted friend that you have potentially been drugged: *"I am not feeling normal. Something isn't right. Stay with me, please. Don't let me out of your sight."* Get out of there immediately.

To the bystander: you might find yourself at a party and hear a group of guys talking about the date rape drug. Then, one of them pulls a tiny bag out of his pocket and shows the goods to everyone in the circle. While all of his buddies may laugh and approve, you know what you're witnessing is wrong and dangerous for someone else. You might even see him prey on a specific young lady at the party and drop a pill in her drink. As he slips into the corner of the room to wait for the drug to enter her system, you have a responsibility to step up and protect that young woman. To stand by and watch the coward's plan unfold is cowardly of you. No matter what, don't ever knowingly allow this to happen. Put a stop to it.

To the offender, if you are tempted at any point to drug a young woman and satisfy your sexual desires on her lifeless body — shame on you. The belief that sex is your right as a man, and a woman is nothing more than an object for you to use as you please, is one of the most unreasonable, disgusting, immoral mindsets a human could ever possess. If a young, hardly-dressed woman entices you, hangs all over you at a party and even whispers provocative things in your ear — that is not equivalent to her consent to knock her unconscious with a pill and rape her. Furthermore, it will mentally haunt you the rest of your life. I'm confident you don't want to live the rest of your life knowing you did such a despicable thing to someone. So don't do it.

CHAPTER 55

Addiction

"Addiction is when you can't get enough of what you don't want anymore." — Deepak Chopra

The Center on Addiction offers this definition of addition: "a complex disease, often chronic in nature, which affects the functioning of the brain and body. It also causes serious damage to families, relationships, schools, workplaces, and neighborhoods. The most common symptoms are severe loss of control, continued use despite consequences, preoccupation with using, and failed attempts to quit."[60]

Over 40 million Americans ages 12 or older — or more than 1 in 7 people — abuse or are addicted to nicotine, alcohol, or other drugs. That is more than the number of Americans with heart conditions (27 million), diabetes (26 million) or cancer (19 million).[61]

Addiction ruins more lives than just the addict's. It breaks families down emotionally, mentally, and financially. It is a disease and it is a thief. It shows up many times in college with casual enjoyment of drugs and alcohol, but then it lingers for decades, resulting in unemployment, divorce, fractured families, bankruptcy, felonies, time behind bars, and even death.

Just…

Be…

Careful.

PART SEVEN

RELATIONSHIPS

A relationship is *the way in which two or more concepts, objects, or people are connected.* In 1929, a Hungarian journalist Frigyes Karinthy released his "Six Degrees of Separation Theory," which states that all living people are six or fewer relationships away from each other. So, a chain of "a friend of a friend" statements can be made to connect any two people in the entire world in a maximum of six steps. The theory is hard to believe, but then again, I get on Instagram and frequently see a groomsman from my wedding out to dinner with President Donald Trump! There you have it — two relationship steps away from the President of the United States! If you can believe it, I also had an elderly taxi driver once who lived in one of Mother Teresa's orphanages and made breakfast with her on numerous occasions.

Relationships can be fun, healthy, tense, hard, smooth, difficult, annoying, exhausting, complicated, fulfilling, strong, fractured, and so on. They can build you up or weigh you down. They can be frustratingly one-sided. They can be short lived or last a lifetime.

Relationships can unexpectedly appear, too.

I once told a total stranger that he could park his big rig in our church parking lot overnight and let his elephants get out and stretch their legs. Yes, he was traveling across the country with elephants. We became friends so quickly that he stopped by the church again on his way back home. This time, however, the elephants didn't get to leisurely and quietly stroll around the field. We invited our college ministry to arrive early that night for elephant rides. We actually took Vicki, a 40-year-old Asian elephant, inside the church and up on the stage. I preached the first part of my sermon that night sitting on top of an elephant.

My wife and I landed in Los Angeles one time, loaded our bags into a trunk, and headed to the hotel. On that 45-minute drive, we got to know our cab driver and heard quite a bit of his story. We exchanged numbers and hired him to drive us the rest of the week. We continued to text each other over the next few months, and then we bought him a flight to Oklahoma to hang out for a few days. Not kidding. When he arrived, he told me, *"This is the strangest thing ever…flying to Oklahoma to hang out with someone I barely know. When you invited me, I thought you could be a serial killer."* That's the first time my over-friendliness has been speculated as potentially deadly. This guy is still a friend today, and he actually stopped by our house for dinner last year as he drove through Oklahoma.

On a train in Morocco, a man sat down next to me. An hour later, we knew about one another's family and were sharing an interesting conversation about the differences between the Bible and the Qur'an. When it was time to exit the train, we felt our conversation wasn't over. So, we went and enjoyed a hot tea and some nasty fried bread together. The unforgettable conversation we shared that day far exceeds the price of the train ticket (as well as the price I paid for eating that fried bread).

In a parking lot one day, I heard laughter that I wanted to bottle up and keep forever. I approached a strikingly adorable 76-year-old woman to thank her for her infectious laugh. Noticing the little girl next to her, I asked her to introduce me to her granddaughter. She told me, "Honey, she's not my granddaughter. She's my foster daughter." A 76-year-old widow—fostering children. Drawn to her story, Andrea and I took her to lunch. Her son was in the hospital, so we went there together, too. This dear woman is so dear to my heart and her story is food for my soul. For her age, she does exceptionally well texting with Emojis, too.

Elephants, taxis, trains, and parking lots. Relationships are everywhere and just waiting to happen. Be ready, be open, and be willing.

CHAPTER 56

Friendship

"Life is slippery. Here, take my hand." — Jackson Brown, Jr.

Have you noticed how our culture is progressively supportive of aggressive self-expression? If you hate someone, say it. If you disagree with something, say it. If you oppose an idea, say it. And say it loud and proud. Post it all over the Internet. At a very young age, we discover an instinctive desire to win and succeed. Success, of course, is measured by achievement and status. The questions become: *"Can I get what I want out of life, how quickly can I get it, and who is in my way?"* Unfortunately, this mindset quickly bleeds into our friendships and causes our friendships to bleed.

Even the disciples of Jesus—the dudes that walked closely with the Man with the purest heart in the world—were bit by the bug of winning. In Mark 10, James and John ask Jesus: *"Can you do something for us? We want to be awarded the highest places of honor. Can we sit to your right and your left?"* Now, I agree, the best seat in the house is the one next to Jesus. But still, who asks that? We read that the other ten disciples lost their tempers, maybe because they thought James and John asked an unfair question, or because they were jealous that they didn't ask first!

Jesus calms them all down with a firm rebuke: *"Guys,*

whoever wants to become great must also learn to serve. If you want to be first, you must learn to be a slave. Look at me — I'm not here to be served, but to serve, and give my life." (Mark 10:43-45, paraphrase) That's a pretty interesting, counter-cultural, pride-shattering reversal of our instincts.

Abraham Maslow, one of the great thinkers of the twentieth century, brought a radical shift of perspective to modern psychology. In his research, he studied people who were vitally alive, radiant, fully-functioning, and genuinely happy people. His conclusion of the secret of this life of vitality is this: *"Without exception, I found that every person who was sincerely happy and radiantly alive was living for the purpose and cause of others."*[62] So according to Jesus and Maslow, it appears that prioritizing others will result in a life of great internal blessing and peace. Worth trying, right?

To be a good friend, I think, is to follow the instructions Paul sent to one of the first churches around: *"Do nothing out of selfish ambition or vain conceit. Rather, in humility value others above yourselves, not looking to your own interests but each of you to the interests of others."* (Philippians 2:3-4) Want to be good friend? Discover ways that you can help and serve your friends. And not just when it is convenient. Instead, deliberately choose to serve when it is an inconvenience to you. And don't worry about getting credit. Just be a good friend and look out for someone else's interest before your own!

Let me offer one more thought that will save you a headache or two when it comes to friendship. This is extremely old advice from a first century Jewish philosopher, Philo Alexander: *"Be kind, because everyone you meet is fighting a great battle."* Our friendships are healthier when we remember that everyone we know is struggling in some way. *Everyone!* Think of each of your friends like an iceberg. Only 10% of an actual iceberg is visible above the water. The rest is unseen, reaching deep into the cold, dark waters of the ocean. We only see the *tip of the iceberg*. Similarly, you may only know 10% of what's going on in your friend's life. Underneath what's visible, I promise you, are many hidden struggles. You will probably have a friend at some point that is suffering with crippling depression or anxiety. A friend that is deeply disappointed about something. A friend that can't afford to fly home for the holidays. Or doesn't want to. A friend that gets addicted to drugs or alcohol. A friend that watches his or her parents walk through a nasty divorce. A friend that gets cancer. A friend that is sexually assaulted. A friend that repeatedly makes poor choices to mask severe insecurities. A friend that is suicidal. Don't rush to conclusions based off of the 10% you know about your friends.

Instead, as Eugene Peterson translates Philippians 2: "Love each other. Be deep-spirited friends. Don't push your way to the front; don't sweet-talk your way to the top. Put yourself aside, and help others get a head. Don't be obsessed with getting your own advantage. Forget about yourselves long enough to lend a helping hand."[63]

It takes a lifetime to master the art of being a good friend and forgetting about yourself, so now is a good time to start practicing.

CHAPTER 57

Red Flags

"Comparison is the thief of joy."
— Theodore Roosevelt

I realize the previous chapter on friendship set the bar high. Relax, your relationships will never be perfect and will require constant work and attention. That being said, let me offer a few red flags to help steer you in the right direction and potentially avoid some relational casualties:

1. Isolation

    Someone once said, *"Isolation violates the laws of the human nature as much as trying to breath under water."* In other words, if you intend on walking through life alone, it is no different than jumping off of the high dive, swimming to the bottom of the pool, and taking a deep breath. It doesn't work. You are meant to have relationships, so avoiding them is risky. Isolation is dangerous. From the Bible, we learn "Whoever isolates himself seeks his own desire; he breaks out against all sound judgment." (Proverbs 18:1) Have you ever seen how sea otters sleep? If you haven't, you should probably Google it because it's adorable. These cute little mammals link their hands with one another, often in a group as large as one hundred. These groups are called "rafts," and they are essential in keeping them safe as they drift around the coast of the Northern Pacific Ocean. They link arms so they don't drift away. Don't isolate yourself. Don't run the risk of drifting away. Get in a raft of people and link up!

2. Insincerity

Avoid the superficial and surface-level tendency of relationships. Artificial friendship is often birthed when one person uses another. First of all, don't use someone for your own gain or advancement. But also watch out for others who might use you. This is the "what's in it for me" mentality. My kids still use the "BFFL" terminology (Best Friends For Life) to describe their unbreakable bond with someone. You'll quickly learn that many college students operate with the "BFFN" mentality: Best Friends For Now. If you begin to notice a superficial tone to one of your relationships, either have a serious heart-to-heart and figure out what's wrong, or invest your time and energy elsewhere.

3. Comparison

For the rest of your life, you'll fight the temptation to compare yourself with others. After college, you'll notice more and more what people drive, where they live, where they work, where they vacation, how they appear, and you can even guess what they're worth. Be careful not to start this habit of comparison in college. Comparison can quickly damage relationships, and I assure you, it will steal your joy in a heartbeat.

4. Gossip

"Did you hear what happened?" "Did you hear what he said?" "Did you hear what he did?" Blah, blah, blah. I'm telling you, one of the most divisive moves you can make is to talk about someone behind their back. We all have experience to some degree with this nasty relational weapon. People have talked about me behind my back, and it hurt. Unfortunately, I've gossiped before, and it hurt others.

The best way I've ever heard this challenged is from St. Augustine, who had the following words etched into his wooden dining table: "Whoever thinks that he is able to nibble at the life of absent friends must know that he is unworthy of this table." His standards are wise to follow.

5. Drama

For the most part, this is pinned on women. But, we all know guys can be whiny, emotional little brats, too. In all my years of marriage, I have never seen my wife speak or act dramatically. Is she a real person who has emotions, loses her temper and overreacts? Sure. But she doesn't create or tolerate drama. On the contrary, we've had friends who turn everyday situations into soap operas. While Andrea lets issues roll off of her shoulders like warm butter off of a plate, others seem to wake up with the ambition of lighting dynamite and blowing relationships up. Drama is like dynamite to relationships. At some point, you will experience a friend who is acting borderline insane over something minor. Someone who likes to turn tiny molehills into mountains. Love them well and try to talk them off of the cliff, but whatever you do, don't pour fuel on the fire. Help turn their mountain into a molehill again. By the way, don't claim that you don't like drama, and then go start drama. That's annoying and immature.

6. Difficult People

When we aren't patient, we can easily fall into the trap of magnifying the shortcomings and faults and failures of others. As a result, we live with a short temper and constant irritability. This is especially hard with the "difficult people" in our lives. *We all have them.* You might live with one!! Try your best to discern whether or not someone is being difficult, or just different. We all have diverse temperaments, tastes, habits, and routines. If your roommate gets up earlier than you and occasionally wakes you up as she makes coffee, maybe she's not *difficult* to deal with. She's different. And if she's up early to start her day, she's also driven. Maybe instead of being angry with her, you could learn from her and get your tail out of bed early, too. Try not to look at your own shortcomings with a telescope while looking at the shortcomings of others with a microscope.

By the way — there are difficult people you *deal with*, but you are probably someone else's difficult person, too. So demonstrate patience with them, because someone is constantly trying to be patient with you.

7. Haters.

No matter how good of a friend you are, you will feel opposition at some point from someone. The real test in relationships is when someone else does something harmful to you, your reputation, your possessions, or your well-being. *How do you respond?* Rather than "shake the haters off" (also known as "you're dead to me"), take the higher road. For example:

People are unreasonable, illogical and self-centered. Love them anyway. If you do good, people will accuse you of selfish, ulterior motives. Do good anyway. If you are successful, you will win false friends and true enemies. Succeed anyway. The biggest people with the biggest ideas can be shot down by the smallest people with the smallest minds. Think big anyway. What you spent years building may be destroyed overnight. Build anyway. People really need help, but may attack you if you help them. Help people anyway. Give the world the best you've got, and you'll get kicked in the teeth. Give the world the best you've got anyway. — Kent M. Keith

CHAPTER 58

Dating

"He who finds a wife finds what is good and receives favor from the Lord."— Proverbs 18:22

Your love story will be unique. Everyone's is. You might graduate college, get a good job, travel the world, date around, make money, save money, pay off debt, and then settle down to get married. There's nothing wrong with that. But you might fall in love during your college years. *Like, soon.* That is my story.

I was 19-years-old when I first laid eyes on Andrea. It was the most breathtaking moment of my life and it was love at first site (for me, not her). We were both serving as counselors at Kanakuk Kamps, so there was a bit of a challenge getting to know her — she pulled kids behind a ski boat while I taught basketball. I got creative though and figured it would be good exercise for the basketball players to swim. I would do anything to get to the boat dock and have a few minutes around Andrea (thank you, former campers, for your flexibility and understanding).

After two weeks of casual conversations, I couldn't imagine life without her. Back then, Facebook didn't exist, so to find out if she was single, I had to spit some game and actually use words: "Do you have a boyfriend?" Had she said yes, I would have continued, "I get home from camp in August. Be sure you've broken up with him by then." Luckily, though, she was single at the time.

She left camp one term earlier than I did that summer. I had asked her three or four times for her phone number, but she went home without giving it to me. Off she went to Chicago, leaving my hopes of love in her dust. Maybe she was absolutely terrified by the couple of times I mentioned pursuing her for marriage.

When I got home and didn't have her number, I figured my only chance was to knock on millions of doors in Chicago looking for Andrea Barnholt. Again, social media didn't exist, so the woman of my dreams was close to slipping out of my hands. I couldn't find her. To make matters worse, she definitely wasn't looking for me! This is the absolute pit of despair when it comes to love stories!

Thank God — a surprise came in the mail postmarked from heaven: the Kanakuk Staff Directory. With urgency, I flipped a few pages and located Andrea's phone number. Actually, it was her parent's home phone and she had already driven back to Kansas for the fall semester of school. I left a message with her parents: "This is Adam. I met your daughter at Kanakuk this summer and would love to speak with her. Can you please pass on this message to her?"

Thank God (again) — Donna *(my favorite mother-in-law)* called her daughter and relayed the message. Two days later, my phone rang. We arranged to meet in person, where I expressed my desire to pursue her. Her response: "Thank you."

"Thank you?" I was hoping for, "Adam, please, pursue me!" Refusing to give up, I modified my game and kept trying. With the help of God, Kanakuk, and Donna, I eventually got to marry the woman of my dreams. To this day, I still wake up and pinch myself every morning to make sure it isn't all a dream.

Not a single relationship over the course of your life will ever have as much value as the one you have with your spouse. You will experience life's greatest peaks and valleys together. You will laugh and fight. You will work and play. You will know one another's greatest joys and most frustrating insecurities. I share my story of meeting Andrea with you because it happened my sophomore year of college. Your love story could be right around the corner, too.

CHAPTER 59

Diversity

"Diversity may be the hardest thing for a society to live with, and perhaps the most dangerous thing for a society to be without." — William Coffin, Jr.

You live in a pluralistic society. That is, a place in which two or more groups, principles, and sources of authority coexist. Of all places, college almost promises you a seat next to someone very different than you. You will be surrounded by people who do not look, think, talk, worship, or act like you do. While our society mostly paints diversity as a racial issue, here are some cultural and personal elements that you will see coexisting while in college:

- Religion (Christian, Catholic, Muslim, Hindu, Buddhist and more)
- Race (Red and Yellow, Black and White)
- Age (18-22, and a couple who are nearing 30!)
- Political affiliation (Republican, Democrat, Independent, and don't care)
- Intellectual capacity (Valedictorians and drop outs)
- Socioeconomic status (lower, middle, and upper class, and filthy rich)

- Sexuality (heterosexual, homosexual, bisexual, and unsure)
- Gender (male, female, and unsure)

You have probably heard of a "pecking order." If not, it is the informal term for a hierarchical system of social organization of chickens. This term refers to the way that birds express their dominance. *Who is the top chicken? The bottom chicken? The chickens in-between?* The order usually remains unchallenged unless a bird gets stronger and healthier.

Unfortunately, a pecking order exists in our culture, and it is typically initiated because of diversity. Rather than having conversations and building bridges across our differences, people often try to express dominance instead. You will likely witness this happening on your campus.

Now is the time to evaluate your mindset when it comes to diversity. A resource I highly suggest is the Intercultural Development Inventory, which summarizes and reports your orientations toward cultural differences and commonalities. The link to the IDI, as well as other suggested resources, are in the endnotes.[64] In the meantime, make a concentrated, self-reflective effort at building your intercultural competence. Here are some ideas that could help:

1. Prayer (ask God for friendships that reflect diversity)
2. Training (such as the IDI or local workshops)
3. Theater, Film, and Arts (increase your understanding of other cultures)
4. Classes (enroll in a cross-cultural, ethnic, or gender relations class)
5. Books (read an author of a different race or ethnicity)
6. Travel (go experience a different culture with an attitude to learn)

7. Reflection (explore your family history, your roots, and your privilege)
8. Site Visits (find ways to learn and grow in your own local area)

Lastly, look for diversity and value it. Personally, having a biracial family has resulted in many thoughts, feelings, and experiences I possibly wouldn't have had otherwise. My son's first Christmas with us gave me a lesson I'll never forget. With his broken English, he said, *"Daddy, you white. I black."* I said, *"Andre, when I look at you, I don't see black. I see my son."* That immediately disarmed our differences.

All-American Dad, right?

Wrong.

In that moment, I realized the beauty of diversity, and that our differences should be acknowledged and appreciated. I tried again: *"Andre, I take that back. When daddy looks at you, I do see my son. I also see your black skin. I see it, and I love it. I think it's beautiful. I'm so happy God made you the wonderful way that he did."* I was reminded that day that diversity isn't to be ignored or avoided, but instead, pursued and appreciated.

CHAPTER 60

Mentors

"If your mentors only tell you that you are awesome, it is time to find other mentors." — Cosette Gutierrez

One of the greatest assets to you in this season of your life is to find mentors and submit to their counsel. I encourage you to find men and women you trust who can speak directly into different arenas of your life. For example, you could submit to mentors for spiritual direction, relationship advice, physical accountability, emotional encouragement, or financial guidance. You might also consider a mentor in the area of academics and your career path.

Your mentors don't need to be professional licensed counselors or therapists. There is no training needed on their end. They simply need to know you, care deeply for you, and possess a willingness to invest in your life. Odds are, you already know one or two people who would gladly mentor you.

Mentors are people that should be able to shoot you straight. Therefore, you need to have some thick skin and be able to take some coaching. Be teachable. Submit your questions, challenges, thoughts, and dreams and listen to their response. Bounce ideas off of them. But be careful — if you pick mentors who love you so much that they refuse to admit your poop stinks, you'll probably never learn anything worthwhile from them. These people need to be your fans, but also your loving critics.

When I was in my mid-20s, I had some serious disagreements with a boss. Young, stubborn, and prideful, I called a mentor of mine and gave him an earful about all the poor leadership qualities I saw in my boss, as if it were my job to fix the guy. Now, over a decade later, I still remember my mentor's advice. He said, "Adam, agreement isn't the same as submission. You don't have to agree with your boss, but you do have to submit to him. God is watching to see if you will honor your boss and work faithfully under his supervision, even if you disagree with his leadership."

In the moment, I remember being frustrated. I wanted to feel heard. *"Wow, Adam, that sounds terrible. You should quit immediately!"* Instead, I was told to submit and serve with honor. Thanks to that mentor's willingness and ability to call me out, the trajectory of my ministry path has been blessed. I am so grateful that my mentor refused to be soft and sensitive with me. Instead, his honesty and wisdom protected me from what could have become a vocational train wreck.

Lastly, please be above reproach in the people you select to mentor you. For example, young ladies shouldn't pursue married men as mentors and then meet with them alone in their office or a coffee shop. Be wise and careful, as submission to authority figures can result in a somewhat close relationship with intimate, personal dialogue. I have multiple mentors in my life and none of them are women. I wholeheartedly believe in a woman's capacity to be a leader. I frequently learn new things from wise women! But there is only one woman I share intimate details with regarding my life, and you already know who she is.

CHAPTER 61

Family

*"Families are like fudge – mostly sweet
with a few nuts."* — Les Dawson

There might be a horrifying moment for you in college when you're looking for an adult to help you with something, and then you realize that *you are an adult.* So then you look for an older adult — someone who seems more experienced in "adulting." Or, you could just call your mom or dad. Or a grandparent. Or older sibling.

Sure, your dad might be full of irrelevant advice and want to tell stories of his college years (which might be unhelpful and totally boring). And your mom, good Lord, she might be all up in your business, demanding a play by play of everything you've done for the last 96 hours, not giving sound advice, but telling you how to live your life. Still, they are your parents. You might think they are nuts *(and you might be right)*, but no offense, you probably didn't fall very far from the family tree.

Give them a break and give them a call. More often than not, they're waiting by the phone just to hear your voice and hear you're doing ok. And more often than not, if you ask them to listen and give their advice, it usually ends up being very helpful.

CHAPTER 62

The Golden Rule

*"Do to others what you would have them
do to you."* — Jesus (Matthew 7:12)

You've heard of the "Golden Rule." There are many theories of the origin of this rule. Most believable, and my personal favorite, is a claim from the third-century Roman Emperor Alexander. He was super impressed with the Christian principle of treating others how you want to be treated. As a result, he had the phrase from Matthew 7:12 inscribed on the gold wall of his chamber![65]

I could simplify this for you: *don't be rude.*

Here are a few practical applications of the Golden Rule that you could try:

Don't seek revenge. Don't bear grudges. Don't allow the seed of resentment to grow in your heart. Look after the other person's well-being. Visit the sick. Pray for those who make you mad. Share what you have with others. Eagerly look for opportunities to serve. Control your tongue. Don't gossip or slander or insult others. Be tenderhearted and kind to others. Forgive quickly. Desire to give rather than receive. Be patient. Put aside envy and pride. Don't celebrate when others fail to succeed. Listen well when others talk. Believe the best in others. Love deeply.

One night, a family in our church was grieving the loss of a loved one. The same night, we attended an event to celebrate my daughter's graduation from elementary school. I said, *"Ellie, you know you are more important to me than ministry, but right now, a family is really hurting. Would it be ok if I left to go be with that family?"* Ellie looked at me and said, *"Daddy, I'm happy right now and they aren't. You need to be with them."* The Golden Rule.

The Golden Rule is easier said than done, but that's no excuse. You won't always get it right, but always give it your best attempt. Others deserve it, whether it is reciprocated or not.

CHAPTER 63

Conflict Resolution

"Conflict is inevitable but combat is optional." — Max Lucado

You've probably heard the "Serenity Prayer," which reads: *"God, grant me the strength to accept the things I cannot change; courage to change the things I can; and wisdom to know the difference."* A modified version of this prayer that you might occasionally relate to is: *"God, grant me the strength to accept the things I cannot change; courage to change the things I can, and forgiveness when I finally snap and go off on someone."*

You're going to snap every once in a while. One of my college roommates pushed the limits of my patience. He liked to make eggs and toast in the mornings (it would have been awesome if he followed the Golden Rule and made breakfast for all of his roommates, too, but whatever). On multiple occasions, he'd go to class after his continental breakfast and leave the stove top on. Before you think, "That's not a huge deal," let me clarify — this happened more than 20 times. I'd tell the dude he needed to turn the stove top off. "Ok," he'd say, glaring at me as if it weren't a big deal and as if house fires weren't a real thing. One morning, I walked into the kitchen to find a towel lying on the stovetop. It was on fire. Now, I was hot (literally and figuratively). This is entirely unacceptable, as his daily appetite for eggs and toast could have resulted in firemen delivering my charcoal remains to my family. This was no longer safe and we had to talk.

The authors of a book called *Crucial Conversations* define one as a "discussion between two or more people where stakes are high, opinions vary, and emotions run strong."[66] Ok, let me break this definition down for you in this particular scenario with my roommate:

1. Stakes were high (the place could have burned down).
2. Opinions varied (he didn't think it was a big deal).
3. Emotions ran strong (I was ready to rumble).

The same authors mentioned above claim that "all strong relationships, careers, organizations, and communities draw from the same source of power — the ability to talk openly about high-stakes, and emotional, controversial topics."[67] Whether you have an issue with your roommate's dangerous cooking habits, your parents, professors, teammates, a boyfriend or girlfriend — conflict is best resolved when you wait until your temper calms down, and then you initiate a conversation. If you talk calmly, you'll be surprised how often the outcome is in favor of both parties. As writer Ambrose Bierce puts it, *"If you speak when you are angry, you will make the best speech you will ever regret."*

Lastly, practice the art of listening. The very worst conflict resolution is when one person does all the talking and never listens. David Dean Rusk was the United States Secretary of State from 1961-1969 under Presidents John F. Kennedy and Lyndon B. Johnson. In his role, he served as the senior official of the federal government focusing on foreign affairs. This guy was engaged in conversations on a massive scale, and his advice is timeless: *"One of the best ways to persuade others is with your ears — listen to them."*

You get a free card to flip out if your roommate leaves the stovetop on and almost burns the place down. Otherwise, resolve your conflict like a big boy or a big girl. Learning to do so now in college is great training for your marriage and career. You won't always get along perfectly with your spouse and boss. Not a chance. So start practicing healthy conflict resolution today!

CHAPTER 64

Forgiveness

"To forgive is to set a prisoner free and to discover the prisoner was you."— Lewis Smedes

M ost of the time, conflict resolution involves some sort of shared responsibility. Sometimes you're 50% at fault and the other person is 50% at fault. Even if it is 99% vs. 1%, that's still shared responsibility to resolve conflict.

Unfortunately, there will be times when another person is 100% responsible for hurting you and you are 100% innocent. As the victim, it is not always appropriate or necessary to schedule coffee with the other person to resolve conflict face to face. However, it needs to be dealt with internally. Conflict resolution in some cases is more about the victim deciding in his or her heart to forgive the other person. In the event that you are severely hurt (any kind of abuse), forgiveness isn't about giving your offender what they deserve. *Of course they don't deserve to be forgiven!* Forgiving that person is about giving your own soul what it needs.

The Bible instructs us: "Do not repay anyone evil for evil. Be careful to do what is right in the eyes of everybody. If it is possible, as far as it depends on you, live at peace with everyone. Do not take revenge, my friends, but leave room for God's wrath, for it is written: 'It is mine to avenge; I will repay,' says the Lord." (Romans 12:17-19) Of course, when we are hurt, our instinct is to slip into self-preservation mode and attack back. However, there is a better way. For the sake of peace, we should commit our concerns to God's hands and not our own.

In only 100 days (April 7 to mid-July, 1994), members of the Hutu ethnic majority in the east central African nation of Rwanda murdered almost one million people. I've been to Rwanda twice, and have visited the Kigali Genocide Memorial Center. The couple of hours I've spent there are etched into my brain forever. I saw images and heard stories of the genocide that are haunting.

During these trips, I learned that the nation has been revitalized by the power of forgiveness. What was once a desolate land full of inconceivable stories of pain and suffering, is now a country taking pride in reconciliation. Immaculée Ilibagiza's book, *Left to Tell*, stretched my understanding of forgiveness to unimaginable levels. After the genocide, Immaculée visited her hometown and met the man who murdered her mother and brother. She writes: *"His name is Felicien. He was sobbing. I could feel his shame. He looked up at me for only a moment, but our eyes met. I reached out, touched his hands lightly, and quietly said what I'd come to say: 'I forgive you.'"* Immaculée shares the reaction of another man present that day: "What was that all about, Immaculée? That was the man who murdered your family. I brought him to you to question, to spit on if you wanted to. But you forgave him! How could you do that? Why did you forgive him?" She answered: *"Forgiveness is all I have to offer."*[68]

Immaculée is a great example of the power of forgiveness, but also an example of a woman who has been healed from the cancer of anger. To forgive is to be merciful, and Matthew 5:7 tell us, "Blessed are the merciful, for they will be shown mercy." Mercy is compassion or forgiveness shown toward someone who you have the power to punish or harm. Choose mercy, and you will be blessed!

PART EIGHT

SPIRITUALITY

When you reach your 30s, your metabolism will slow down, your joints will start to hurt a little, and you'll be sorer after physical activities. Although I'm still *somewhat* young, I understand the value of taking daily vitamins. I take a daily men's vitamin that gives me the necessary nutrients that will keep my body and immune system healthy. I take a daily antihistamine to help with my allergies (you'd understand if you ever visited northeast Oklahoma, which is also known as *Green Country).* I also take a daily capsule of Omega-3 fish oil, which supports heart health and helps reduce discomfort or swelling in my joints (because playing basketball with my four kids isn't as easy as it used to be). These pills sit by my bathroom sink and give me easy, daily access to a healthier life.

There isn't a pharmacy in the world that can put spirituality in a capsule. In other words, God is not a pill. We can't think of him once a day, gulp him down with a drink of water and subconsciously absorb him through our gut. If it were that easy, Christianity would be cheap and shallow. Part 8 is about spiritual transformation. See, popping a daily allergy pill doesn't transform my allergies. It certainly helps by treating symptoms and lowering my discomfort. But to fix my allergies, I need entirely new sinuses. Spiritually speaking, Jesus gives us a new heart. That, my friend, is transformation.

In this book, I've offered insights on your identity, maturation process, academics, money, sex, alcohol, relationships, and your future. But, as you may imagine, this chapter deals with what I find most important in life: your relationship with Jesus.

Without knowing where you stand in your spiritual life, please read this chapter slowly and take time to ponder these topics. Many young people fall into the mistake of understanding Christianity as a brief, casual prayer that secures a seat in heaven. Author Richard Foster argues this perspective well. He says, *"The goal of the Christian life is not simply to get us into heaven, but to get heaven into us!" God is not seeking to improve us, but to transform us."*[69] I believe your college years can very much be a time of transformation.

Do you?

CHAPTER 65

Discovery

*"You will seek me and find me when you seek
me with all your heart."* — Jeremiah 29:13

As a youth and college pastor, I've taken thousands of students to summer camps and retreats. While there, students are free from the temptations back home, the comparisons seen on social media, and the stresses of living up to the expectations of their parents. In settings like these, young people experience a "spiritual high" (sort of like smoking a religious joint). Students often returned home with vows to improve their behavior, make better choices, stop messing around sexually, read their Bible daily, and absolutely never, ever, no matter what happens, miss another church service as long as they live.

Because that's what Christianity is all about, right? *Performance?*

Wrong.

Pledging to *be better* doesn't work out that well for most students, because eventually the high wears off. Unfortunately, in most of these cases, young people over promise and under deliver.

My challenge to you during your college years isn't to *be better,* but to *discover more.* Discover more about God and yourself. Part of the discovery process is to ask tough questions.

Author Caroline Westerhoff says, *"Our danger lies in questioning too little rather than too much. After all, our questions can be the voice of God."*[70] Whether the message of Christ has been spoon fed to you since you were in diapers, or the gospel of Jesus is brand spanking new, get busy discovering more. Keep in mind that part of His nature is incredibly mysterious. Therefore, find a reliable, God-fearing person or source and ask questions that will help you discover more about God. He already knows what your questions are, so ask away...

CHAPTER 66

Ownership

*"Examine yourselves as to whether you are
in the faith…"* — 2 Corinthians 13:5

My generous in-laws took my wife and I and our four children to Disneyland. What an experience! The night before our departure, my wife surprised our family of six with matching t-shirts for the trip. Listen, I love my wife. *I adore her. She's amazing.* But, as you can imagine, I was not excited about these shirts. Not excited at all. I lovingly and tenderly pushed back. I said something like, *"Why do we have to wear these stupid shirts?"* By the way, the shirts said, "WE ARE FAMILY." Of course we are a family — we are sitting on the same row of chairs, waiting at the same gate, for the same airplane, in the same airport. Everyone knows we are a family. Why do our shirts need to reinforce the absolute obvious? (You already know that my wife won — she gave me one glare and I put that shirt on.)

Be careful not to put on someone else's spirituality. Your faith story needs to be your story, and while others can influence and lead you in a positive way, Jesus wants to write your story as unique and different than everyone else's. Be you and own your faith story. The faith of your parents and the teaching of your youth pastor can point you in a good direction, but they can't reconcile you with our sovereign God.

Your relationship with Jesus isn't meant to match someone else's like my family's matching t-shirts. Simply put, you have to possess ownership of your own heart in order to transfer that ownership to Jesus. No one else can make that transaction for you. If you haven't done so, what are you waiting for?

CHAPTER 67

The Trinity

*"May the grace of the Lord Jesus Christ, and
the love of God, and the fellowship of the Holy
Spirit be with you all."* — 2 Corinthians 13:14

The Triune nature of God is one of the most perplexing
concepts to comprehend. Christians profess faith in "one
God," yet the Bible reveals there are three: Father, Son, and Holy
Spirit. To keep this short, I'll briefly summarize the nature of
the Trinity, and the collective work of the three Persons.

In the Greek, *perichoresis* is the term used to describe the
Triune nature of God, and the relationship can be understood as
co-indwelling. Author Alister McGrath writes that the Trinity
*"allows the individuality of the Persons to be maintained, while
insisting that each person shares in the life of the other two. An
image often used to express this idea is that of a 'community of
being,' in which each person, while maintaining its distinctive
identity, penetrates the others and is penetrated by them."*[71] It
is helpful to think of the three Persons of the Trinity as being
infiltrated and permeated by the others.

People typically associate each Person of the Trinity with
specific stories in the Bible and particular roles in the life of
a Christian. For example, many credit "God the Father" for
Creation. However, the Hebrew people knew God to be more

than a solo-artist in the sky. Genesis 1:26 reveals the plural nature of God: "Then God said, 'Let *us* make man in *our* image, in *our* likeness…'"

Sure, God created us. But Jesus Christ and the Holy Spirit are equally responsible for creation. God is three Persons, and all three Persons have the same essence of deity. Our finite minds try to define the Trinity as $1 + 1 + 1 = 3$, but really, we should understand the Father, Son and Holy Spirit as $1 \times 1 \times 1 = 1$. The meaning of Trinity is a combination of two concepts: *tri* (three) + *unity* (one). Three in one. If this is making your head hurt, that's ok. Explaining and understanding the Trinity gives academic scholars migraines. That's why you can't fully explain the mystery of God. You simply have to trust Him and experience Him.

CHAPTER 68

The Problem

"For all have sinned and fallen short of
the glory of God." — Romans 3:23

We are created in the image of God to have relationship with God. However, in the very beginning, humanity faced a choice: obey God or disobey God. Because of the disobedience of Adam and Eve, we are all born into sin, and when we grow up, we choose to sin. The world is full of total depravity and corruption, and no one is exempt. Unfortunately, the slightest sinful decision can cause massive destruction to your life.

I once returned home from Africa without knowing I was carrying a very rare and merciless parasite called Cryptosporidium Parvum. One night, I was sitting on the couch and felt an unbearable pain in my abdomen. The next morning, I consulted with my doctor and he shared with me a plan to wipe out the parasite village in my gut. This parasite was invisible to the naked eye, yet it controlled my life for over a month. It determined what I ate. It caused me to miss work. And it kept me within close proximity to a restroom (I was nervous to even trust a toot). Something so miniscule took total control of my life.

Sin is no different.

The very smallest, insignificant sin can result in giant consequences. The greatest consequence is that our sin separates us from God. And if our sinful nature isn't dealt with in this life, we miss out on eternal life with the Lord. That is why the Bible refers to our need for a Savior, a Redeemer, a Deliverer. We need to be saved and redeemed and delivered. Our sin is gross, and we need help. A lot of help.

We have an enemy. His name is Satan. He is constantly attempting to demolish your life and mine. Jesus actually said our enemy's aim is to "steal, kill and destroy" each and everyone one of us (John 10:10). In 1 Peter 5:8, Satan is described as a lion: *"Be self-controlled and alert. Your enemy the devil prowls around like a roaring lion looking for someone to devour."* Do you know why lions roar? To express severe hunger pangs and to intimidate their prey. Our enemy is hungry and he wants to tear apart your life. However, with God's help, the intimidating roar of a lion is turned into a pathetic little cry of a kitty cat.

If you read Romans 8:5-11, you'll see that we are all going to wrestle with our sinful nature. In the Greek, "sinful nature" can be understood as one who is infected by the lust of the flesh *(phronema sarkos)*. When we are controlled by our flesh, we stand in opposition to the principles of God. When we walk in sin, we are incompatible with true life, and peace in our souls is impossible.

So what do we do?

First, let go of your past. Sure, you've made mistakes. Your life has certainly not measured up to perfection. Romans 8:1 promises that there is no condemnation for those who are in Christ Jesus. Don't allow the enemy to crucify you on the cross of your mistakes from yesterday.

Second, be honest with yourself. Take a scan of your heart and mind and determine if something has control over you.

If you ignore, deny, or lie about your sinful nature, you are only digging a deeper hole for your soul. I love how David invited God: "Search me, God, and know my heart; test me and know my anxious thoughts. See if there is any offensive way in me, and lead me in the way everlasting." (Psalm 139:23-24) Some translations of that verse say "detestable" instead of "offensive." Our sin is hateful, despicable, and awful. The sooner we recognize and admit that, the sooner we can truly understand our need for redemption.

Thank God — there is an invitation to a process of redemption and restoration. Let's talk about God's solution for our sin.

CHAPTER 69

The Solution

"For God so loved the world that he gave his one and only Son, that whoever believes in Him shall not perish but have eternal life." — John 3:16

Jesus came to earth. Come on! The magnitude of those four words — JESUS CAME TO EARTH — should shake you to your core. Christmas isn't just a holiday. It is the celebration of a rescue mission. Matthew 1:21 tells us that a young virgin woman gave birth to a Son, Jesus, who will save his people from their sins.

The life of Jesus could be classified as amazingly, surprisingly, remarkably, outstandingly extraordinary! He was God in the flesh (John 1) and the greatest teacher (Matthew 7). He performed miracles (Mark 1) and lived a sinless life (Hebrews 4). He set a perfect example (Ephesians 5) and fulfilled all righteousness (Matthew 3). He revealed God to mankind, taught the truth, fulfilled the Law, brought peace, offered a new Kingdom, showed us how to live, healed the sick, and defended the poor. But despite all he accomplished with His life, there was still a price to be paid for our sins: death (see Romans 6:23). Ultimately, Jesus was born to die. To be charged with our transgressions. To give his life as a ransom for many.

I love how C.S. Lewis once said it, "The Son of God became a man so that men might become sons of God."

You probably know John 3:16 — *For God so loved the world that he gave his one and only Son, that whoever believes in him shall not perish but have eternal life.* What could possibly be more important than this? What could be more relevant or urgent or meaningful? God loves the world — every man, woman, and child. Those that have lived, are alive now, or will live. The young and old. Every country, city, town, and village. Every race. Every tribe. Every language. The blessed and oppressed. Every atheist, Muslim, Buddhist, Hindu, Jehovah's Witness, Mormon, and Christian Scientist. The slave and the free. The righteous and the wicked. The rich and the poor. The healthy and the sick. God loves everyone.

This is a global mission for all people — an operation of such magnitude that we couldn't begin to comprehend it! And the solution to our sin is to believe in Jesus! We can't earn our salvation. We can't work for it, or be a good enough person, or deserve salvation through our superior intellect or obedience.

The solution to our total depravity is Jesus.

Jesus alone.

CHAPTER 70

Grace

"My grace is sufficient for you..."
— 2 Corinthians 12:9

Author Paul Zahl defines grace as follows: *"Grace is love that seeks you out when you have nothing to give in return. Grace is love coming at you that has nothing to do with you. Grace is being loved when you are unlovable. Grace has everything to do with the lover, not the beloved. It has nothing to do with weights and measures. It has nothing to do with my intrinsic qualities or so-called 'gifts,' whatever they may be. It reflects a decision on the part of the giver, the one who loves, in relation to the receiver, the one who is loved, that negates any qualifications the receiver may personally hold. Grace is one-way love."*[72]

It is almost too good to be true, right? I mess up, God forgives me. I mess up again and He forgives me again... and again and again. Let me clarify — we must have a repentant attitude about the sin in our life. To minimize our sin is to minimize the cross. Our overall tone should shift when we consider what God is offering to us. Grace is free and it is yours. No strings attached.

This is an incredibly hard idea for human beings to grasp: the doctrine of salvation by grace alone. And why? Because we always want to add something to it. We have pride and we want control, so we like to think: *Unless I also _____, I am not saved.* Unless I attend church, worship, read my Bible, live a moral life, keep the Sabbath, tithe 10%, and love my neighbor, there's no way I can be saved! Those are all great things, but incorrect theology. This gift of grace has *nothing to do with us!* We are told in Ephesians 2:8-9, "For it is by grace you have been saved, through faith—and this is not from yourselves, it is the gift of God—not by works, so that no one can boast." See? Not from yourself. This is a one-way transaction! We don't earn it, but God still gives it. It is all about Him!

I encourage you to go read Luke, chapter 15, where you will see a beautiful depiction of "one way love" in the relationship between a father and a son. To briefly summarize, a young man completely dishonors his father's name, ruins his life, and ends up helpless and starving; then, he heads home to apologize, hoping his dad will at least give him a place to stay. While rehearsing his apology and accepting his reputation as a total failure, his daddy welcomes him home with open arms.

He throws a homecoming party.

God is the Father.

You are the son.

The party awaits.

That's grace.

Don't try to fully understand it. God's grace is a great mystery. Just receive it. Jump in the deep end of the pool of God's grace and swim around in it for a while.

CHAPTER 71

Salvation

*"Yet to all who did receive him, to those
who believed in his name, he gave the
right to become children of God —
children born not of natural descent, nor
of human decision or a husband's will,
but born of God." —* John 1:12-13

Legalism and moralism view Christianity as a moral code. This mindset conveys the message: if you *behave*, you belong. Jesus brings a different message: if you *believe*, you belong. The offer Jesus makes is to exchange your old self (sinful) for a new person (righteous). He offers to make you a new creation. Jesus offers you a new birth — a supernatural transformation of character. A fresh, unused, original creation.

Have you ever fully understood the metamorphosis of a butterfly? Me either, so I went and studied what truly happens. A caterpillar begins as an egg. After hatching, it has one focus: eat, and eat, and eat. When it matures, it starts spinning a silken pad called a chrysalis around its body. What happens in the cocoon is profound and mysterious. All of the cells of the caterpillar turn off, one by one. The larva slowly dissolves from its former worm-like state into an unrecognizable substance until it dies. Within this liquid substance, dormant cells activate and begin to work. These new cells begin building wings, and legs, and eyes, and so on. According to biologists, the change from caterpillar to butterfly is the creation of a *new creature*. Nothing from the old is a part of the new.

Similarly, as Paul wrote, "Therefore, if anyone is in Christ, the new creation has come: The old has gone, the new is here!" (2 Corinthians 5:17) Sure, some people prefer the darkness of sin rather than the light of Christ. Those souls will sadly perish and experience eternal death, alienated from God, without hope. But for those who believe in the message of Christ, they will receive eternal life! Life that can see and taste the glory of God and enjoy his creation as he intended us to!

Jesus coming to earth was an act of love. It wasn't an afterthought or last minute emergency plan. Love is the very nature of God. First John 4:8 tells us, "God is love." And love doesn't just come to *fix us*, but to *fulfill us*.

If you haven't surrendered your heart to Jesus, I'm writing to you right here and right now. If you believe the gospel is true, the objective here isn't to "get saved." I'm talking about surrender. To receive God's love—and to love him back—isn't about a feeling. It is about repentance and surrender. It is turning ways to *the way*.

If your pulse is racing a bit because you believe the story of Jesus to be true, but you've never acted upon that faith, take a deep breath. The Christian walk (looking like Jesus and walking in the Spirit) is tough, but salvation (beginning your walk with Jesus) is simpler than you think. Feel free to reach out to a local pastor or simply speak to God whatever is in your heart. As soon as you are ready, here are a few steps that can help:

1. Focus your mind on your Creator and open your heart.
2. Tell God that you believe in Him and that you trust Him.

3. Profess to God that you believe Jesus died for you.
4. Ask for forgiveness for your sins.
5. Thank God for giving you His Holy Spirit.
6. Commit the rest of your days to Him.

If this was the first time you've expressed your belief through prayer, welcome to the family of God! Today is a new beginning! You are a new creation! Enjoy the amazing, mysterious, supernatural miracle of salvation! Also, my email address is in the back of this book. Send me an email so that I can pray for you by name and celebrate with you the decision you've made to trust God!

CHAPTER 72

The Holy Spirit

"If you love Me, you will keep my
commandments. And I will ask the Father,
and He will give you another Advocate to
be with you forever — the Spirit of truth.
The world cannot receive Him, because it
neither sees Him nor knows Him. But you
do know Him, for He abides with you and
will be in you." — Jesus (John 14:15-17)

I'm sometimes jealous of Jesus' disciples. They got to walk with Him and talk with Him. They ate meals together and heard him laugh and listened to him teach in the flesh. They witnessed countless unpredictable and extraordinary moments as they followed. And then, one night at dinner Jesus tells them:

"Now I am going to him who sent me, yet none of you
asks me, 'Where are you going?' Because I have said
these things, you are filled with grief. But I tell you the
truth: It is for your good that I am going away. Unless
I go away, the Counselor will not come to you; but if I
go, I will send him to you." (John 16:5-7)

I bet the disciple's thoughts began to race...
Where did you say you're going, Jesus?
I don't want you to leave us.
I left everything to follow you. Please, Lord, stay.
Who is this Counselor you speak of?

The Counselor is the Spirit of God, who does not walk next to us, but dwells in us. Our bodies are consecrated as temples for the Holy Spirit to live in. This changes everything! At the moment of salvation, you aren't given a list of instructions or a map to follow in order to find God. God comes and lives in you! Let me share with you three wonderful ways the Holy Spirit ministers to us every day.

1. The Holy Spirit counsels us. In John 14:26, we read Jesus telling us, "But the Counselor, the Holy Spirit, whom the Father will send in my name, will teach you all things and will remind you of everything I have said to you."

   The Holy Spirit offers us discernment, direction, guidance, and comfort, but we must surrender in order to receive. Think of the first time you sat down with your academic advisor at school. You didn't tell the professional what classes you wanted to take! You sought and submitted to his or her counsel. How much more should we listen, respond and follow the counsel of the Holy Spirit! His counsel trumps all others.

2. The Holy Spirit convicts us. Jesus promised us in John 16:8, "When He (the Holy Spirit) comes, He will convict the world of guilt in regard to sin and righteousness and judgment."

Because the Spirit lives in us, our bodies are sanctuaries for the Holy Spirit! Too often, we view our bodies as the source of sin, but they are precisely where the Holy Spirit chooses to dwell. If this is true, shouldn't there be a huge difference between the person who has the Spirit of God living inside of him or her and the person who does not? That is the conflict — the Spirit and sin both want control. Paul wrote about this: "For the sinful nature desires what is contrary to the Spirit, and the Spirit what is contrary to the sinful nature. They are in conflict with each other, so that you do not do what you want." (Galatians 5:17) Out of that conflict, conviction is birthed. Plain and simple: if you're up to no good, the Holy Spirit will let you know!

3. The Holy Spirit empowers us. Galatians 5:16 says, "So I say, live by the Spirit, and you will not gratify the desires of the sinful nature."

The Christian is not capable of defeating sin without the help of the Holy Spirit. Be careful to not view Christianity as sin management or behavior modification. Don't be obsessed with controlling your sinful nature; instead, focus on the Holy Spirit. He empowers you to resist sinful desires and provides the fruit necessary to do so: love, joy, peace, patience, kindness, goodness, faithfulness, gentleness, and self-control (Galatians 5:22-23).

Although there are nine "fruits" given by the Spirit, they are to be treated singularly as the "fruit of the Spirit." If you are the temple of God's Spirit, you are given all of the above. Avoid this understanding of how God empowers you:

13% love,
10% joy,
12% peace,
11% patience,
12% kindness,
10% goodness,
11% faithfulness,
10% gentleness, and
11% self-control.

Instead, you're a recipient of every fruit:

100% love,
100% joy,
100% peace,
100% patience,
100% kindness,
100% goodness,
100% faithfulness,
100% gentleness, and
100% self-control.

I don't know about you, but when I'm cruising in the fast lane and a car cuts me off, I instinctively have unkind, ungentle thoughts. Patience – not a chance. Joy? Yah right. I suppose I show a little self-control since I don't run them off of the road. Although, I think about it. My point is that the fruit of the Spirit originates in the Spirit, not in you or me. Trying to be joyful without the help of the Holy Spirit sounds exhausting. Therefore, lean in to Him and ask for His help. It is as easy as whispering this short prayer: "Holy Spirit, help me to be fruitful today."

CHAPTER 73

Prayer

"Devote yourselves to prayer..."
— Colossians 4:2

Oswald Sanders calls prayer a Christian's "vital breath and native air."[73] What a beautiful description! Maybe that's why the Bible tells us to be devoted to prayer and to pray without ceasing. (Colossians 4:2 and 1 Thessalonians 5:17) However, the idea of every single breath being devoted to prayer is a bit daunting. I doubt you think about praying while taking a test, scrolling through Instagram, going to the bathroom, or watching a game (well, if your university's football team needs it, you might pray during games). I think what the Bible is urging us to learn is that we ought to maintain a constant awareness of God's presence and our relationship with Him. You can't go out and look for and find God's Presence. You're in His Presence. Always. Everywhere. So, the hope is for greater awareness.

If prayer is a new practice for you, let me take some pressure off of you. Prayer can feel strange at times. Ideally, prayer is a dialogue between you and God. That means prayer includes both speaking and listening. If you're anything like me, your prayer life can easily slip into a one-way conversation. I have to remind myself often to shut up and listen! Prayer is not a project that you will one day complete and finish. Instead, it is a discipline you will nurture throughout the rest of your life. My grandmother is the most devout Christian woman that I know, and as a 90-year-old, even she has shared with me the challenges of staying focused while praying. All that to say, like physical disciplines, spiritual disciplines require practice too. Cut yourself some slack. Practice and be patient. I assure you, God hears you, and He loves that you're talking with Him!

Let me offer a few definitions of different ways that you can pray. In developing this discipline, it is perfectly acceptable to sit down with this list, a journal, and the timer on your phone. Dedicate 3 minutes to each kind of prayer listed below, and simply talk out loud to God. As you do, write down everything that comes to mind. This will allow you to go back and see everything that flowed from your heart in times of prayer. Give each of these a try:

- Praise: simply tell God how you feel about Him. Speak out the many attributes you love about Him. Example: "God, I praise you! I worship you and honor you! You are wonderful and powerful and worthy!"
- Thanksgiving: look at all God has done for you and state your gratitude through prayer. Example: "Lord, thank you for your love. Thank you for your grace. Thank you for providing for me. I am so grateful for the many promises you fulfill in my life. Where would I be without you?"
- Repentance: stating your sorrow for your sin and asking for forgiveness. Example: "Lord, I am sorry for my sin. I am deeply sorry for the way I spoke and for my actions. I acknowledge my wrongdoing and ask for your grace. Thank you, Lord, for your forgiveness."

- Blessing: ask God for His power and Presence upon a person, place or situation. Example: "Please, God, bless my family. Bless this home with your Presence and bless us with your help during our time of need."
- Intercession: prayer on behalf of others. Example: "Jesus, please heal John of his sickness. Please encourage him during this difficult time. Please, Lord, help all those who are hurting. I'm asking, God, that you be with my mother during her surgery."
- Petition: request for your own life. Example: "God, I need your help in this relationship. Please heal me. I need your wisdom for this decision."

You're not going to believe this, but when I was a child, telephones were plugged into the wall. Seriously. There was a cord, and conversations were transmitted via telephone lines instead of satellites. There was also no such thing as call-waiting. So, if I called a friend who happened to already be on the phone with someone else, I heard a busy signal. It beeped over and over again, telling me that my friend was unavailable. Unreachable.

If you say 4,103,019 prayers over the course of your life, you will never hear a busy signal from God. Not once. So call Him anytime.

CHAPTER 74

Worship

*"Let everything that has breath praise the
Lord. Praise the Lord."* — Psalm 150:6

As a graduate from the University of Oklahoma, I'm used to cheering for a pretty awesome football team. Most OU fans aren't content with a 10-win season or even a conference championship. The University of Oklahoma football team is expected to compete for the National Championship. When they don't, grown men lose their tempers and act like fools.

When OU is winning, fans are worshipping. On Saturdays, around 90,000 of us stand in the stadium, covered in expensive team apparel and scream at the top of our lungs. We are willing to stand in scorching heat or freezing rain to watch a game. We study our team's offensive strategy and memorize player's stats and team records. We can name the top players over the past five decades and even know the head coach's kid's names. We pay absurd amounts of money for parking, food and tickets into the stadium. We raise our hands and shake our fists. We jump and clap and shout. We high five and chest bump one another when we score.

Then comes Sunday morning. We stand still in church, listen to songs, drink our coffee, and worry about what others will think of the way we worship. We barely sing because our throats are too sore from screaming at the football game the day before. See, Saturdays prove that we can worship, but Sundays prove that we tend to worship the wrong object. Football is just an example, but throughout your life, you will face the temptation to worship just about everything but God.

Only God is worthy of our worship. Nothing and no one else.

In the Bible, we are told that true and proper worship is to be a living sacrifice to the Lord (Romans 12:1). In the Old Testament, people could make a sacrifice for the Lord. Now, we *are a sacrifice*. Worship is giving God what He wants: you. Oswald Chambers says, *"We have the idea that we can dedicate our gifts to God. However, you cannot dedicate what is not yours. There is actually only one thing you can dedicate to God, and that is your right to yourself. If you will give God your right to yourself, He will make a holy experiment out of you — and His experiments always succeed. The one true mark of a saint of God is the inner creativity that flows from being totally surrendered to Jesus Christ."*[74]

As a living sacrifice, stay on the altar. Don't think of worship as a brief visit to God on Sunday mornings, but a daily choice to surrender your life to Him.

CHAPTER 75

Love

*"Love the Lord your God with all your heart
and with all your soul and with all your mind
and with all your strength."* — Mark 12:29-30

L ove is hard to define. Maybe it's an intense feeling of deep
affection. Synonyms of love include: intimacy, attachment,
devotion, adoration, worship, passion, desire, yearning, and
infatuation. Certainly, we see love enacted just about every day
in some fashion.

We love our family and our country. We love holidays and
snow days and chocolate and puppies. We look for love, fall in
love, make love, and we love with all our hearts. We fall out of
love. Some people love at first sight. We love to be loved and love
can hurt. Some think love is on ABC on Monday nights when
28 women compete for the love of one bachelor.

Love can be pure and cherished and unconditional, or
complicated and frustrating and hard. No matter what our
ideas and experiences are with love, the Bible tells us how to
love God. 1 John 4:19 reminds us that our love for God is our
response to His deep, intense, inexpressible love for us!

In Mark 12, some religious leaders get into a dialogue with
Jesus and ask him which commandment is most important.
This is a lofty question, as there are 613 commandments in

the Pentateuch *(Genesis, Exodus, Leviticus, Numbers and Deuteronomy)*! The long list of instructions and commands incorporates a variety of topics: relationship with God, temples and priests, sacrifices and rituals, purity, the Sabbath, animals for consumption, festivals, community, idolatry, war, family dynamics, justice, civil liabilities, blasphemy, dietary laws, agriculture, loans and business, treatment of slaves, and forbidden relationships.

"Which one, Jesus, is most important," they asked. *"The most important one,"* answered Jesus, *"is this: 'Hear, O Israel: The Lord our God, the Lord is one. Love Him! Love the Lord your God with all your heart and with all your soul and with all your mind and with all your strength.'"* (Mark 12:29-30)

All your heart.

Your passions, affections, and ambitions all aligning with the Lord.

All your soul.

Your longings and desires centered on connecting with your Savior.

All your mind.

Your thoughts and attitudes and perspectives.

All your strength.

Your physical body, energy and concentration.

The intimidating and overwhelming challenge here, in my opinion, is the word *all.* Not some of your heart, a portion of your soul, a part of your mind and half of your strength.

All.

God is to be supremely, exclusively and earnestly loved by you and me. Obeying this command is not to be an act we perform or a box we check on Sunday mornings, but the very essence of who we are. Our entire life should display allegiance and love for God.

CHAPTER 76

The Bible

*"Your word is a lamp for my feet, a
light on my path."* — Psalm 119:105

The Bible is utterly amazing to read. And it truly offers a variety of genres: action, adventure, comedy, fantasy, mystery, politics, speech, romance, drama, tragedy, suspense, and crime. First Timothy 3:16 tells us that "All Scripture is God-breathed and is useful for teaching, rebuking, correcting and training in righteousness." The Bible is invaluable to Christ-followers. We should read it, study it, chew on it, meditate on it, ponder it, and reflect on it. Reading the Bible with the same intensity and devotion you give your Instagram Story is not the goal. Examine the Bible! Basically, reading your Bible without diligently studying the text is like chewing up your lunch but not swallowing your food. Let me give you a few steps to practice when you read your Bible:

1. Prayer: before reading, ask God to open the eyes of your heart.
2. Observation: what does this passage say?
   a. What is the emphasis of the passage?
   b. Are there any repeated words or ideas?
   c. Are there any "if and then" phrases?

    d.   Recognize any comparisons and contrasts.

    e.   Who are the people in the passage?

    f.   Who is being spoken to?

    g.   What is happening?

    h.   Where is the story taking place?

    i.   When is this happening in time?

3. Interpretation: what does this passage mean? Here you can cross-reference (let scripture interpret scripture by looking at other similar, connected verses in the Bible). As you interpret, acknowledge culture. What is the context? Feel free to consult with trustworthy books and websites to learn more about the Bible. A great starting point would be purchasing *How to Read the Bible for All its Worth* and *How to Read the Bible Book by Book* by Gordon Fee and Douglas Stuart.

4. Application: *what am I going to do now?* When you read God's Word, it should impact your life when you close the cover. Here are a few questions you can ask after reading:

    a.   How does this truth impact my relationship with God?

    b.   How does this truth impact my relationship with others?

    c.   How can this verse/passage be a part of my daily life?

In John 8:31, Jesus is quoted saying, "If you abide in my word, you are truly my disciples." Being a disciple is to be a disciplined learner and relentlessly committed follower of a teacher. Our teacher, Jesus, happened to give us a gift on paper that will help us understand more about him and more about life. To abide in God's Word is to remain there. To never elevate any other truth over Scripture. To never cease to be aware and grateful of its value. To never stop enjoying its goodness. To never trust any other path, but to walk in the light. Jesus is saying that the mark of a true disciple is to endure, and persevere, and keep on remaining in the word. I once heard a pastor say that temporary tastes of God's Word don't make you a Christian, but instead, the mark of a Christian is that we taste, and we stay.

The Bible infuses truth into all arenas of your life. Be drawn to the treasure of its pages. You can trust it to nourish you and guide you. Treat it like the supremely cherished gift that it is. I remember worshipping one night in a village in Liberia. It was incredibly hot, and I think we had been singing for an hour, and I needed water. I put my Bible on the ground so I could get my water bottle out of my backpack. A sweet elderly man tapped my shoulder and lovingly said, "Don't put God's Word on the ground." He handed my Bible back to me and I received his correction. I learned in that moment just how precious God's Word is and should be to us all.

This precious gift is for you. So dig in and stay a while.

CHAPTER 77

Confessions

"For the word of God is living and active, sharper than any two-edged sword, piercing to the division of soul and of spirit, of joints and of marrow, and discerning the thoughts and intentions of the heart." — Hebrews 4:12

When most people hear the word *confession*, they immediately think of someone admitting something they've done wrong. But a confession can also be a declaration, an acknowledgment, a revelation, or an announcement. When it comes to the Bible, you can confess Scripture. In other words, you can speak the Bible over you as a proclamation of truth.

Below you will find some examples of scriptural confessions. Usually, when college students would come to me with a wounded heart or pestering fears, I'd start with scriptural confessions. As a pastor, I can pray, encourage, and affirm, but more important than my counsel is the counsel from the Word of God.

Bookmark this chapter, and if you feel the weight of this world pinning you down, read the following scriptural confessions out loud, over and over again:

I am a child of God now (1 John 3:2). Christ lives in me (Galatians 2:20). I am new in Christ, a new creation. Old things have passed away; behold, all things have become new (2 Corinthians 5:17). My body is a temple of the Holy Spirit, who is in me, whom I have from God (1 Corinthians 6:19). Christ is my life (Colossians 3:4). I have been born again, not of corruptible seed but incorruptible, through the Word of God, which lives and abides forever (1 Peter 1:23). I reckon myself to be dead to sin, but alive to God in Jesus Christ my Lord (Romans 6:11). I am a son/daughter of God through faith in Christ Jesus (Galatians 3:26).

I have been born of God (John 1:13). I am a believer (John 1:11). I am the righteousness of God in Christ (2 Corinthians 5:21). I am an ambassador for Christ (2 Corinthians 5:20). I am made a royal priest unto God (Revelation 1:6). I abide in Jesus' Word. I am really a disciple of Jesus (John 8:31). I am a Christian. I am a disciple of Jesus Christ and I abide in His Word and am His indeed (Acts 11:26). I receive the abundance of grace and the gift of righteousness through the One, Jesus Christ (Romans 5:17).

I am of a chosen generation, a royal priesthood, a holy nation, God's own special possession, that I may proclaim the praises of Him who called me out of darkness into His marvelous light (1 Peter 2:9). I abstain from fleshly lusts, which wage war against my soul (1 Peter 2:11). I am in Christ, a new creation. Old things have passed away; behold, all things have become new. I have put off the old self with its deeds (Colossians 3:9). I am Christ's and have crucified the flesh with its passions and desires. Therefore, I no longer have desire for any kind of impurity or sinful behavior (Galatians 5:19-24).

Apart from Jesus, I can do nothing. He has made a way for me. He has poured out His love into my heart through the Holy Spirit, and I can remain in his love. Through Him, I can bear much fruit (Romans 5:5; John 15:4-5).

The Lord is helping me remain in Him and His living words remain in my heart (John 15:7). Jesus keeps me in His love, which is as great as the love between Him and the Father (John 15:9). The Lord is working in me to do His will, to walk in love and obey, so that I can abide in His love and be His friend. He is teaching me to love others with the love of the Father (John 15:10-14). He is teaching me to love and to abide in the light and never cause anyone to stumble (1 John 2:10). He reminds me always of the Word of salvation (1 John 2:24). He came to take away my sins (1 John 3:5).

The Lord gives me confidence so that I am not ashamed (1 John 2:28). He gives me His Spirit (1 John 4:13). I confess that Jesus is the Son of God, that God abides in me, and I in Him (1 John 4:15).

CHAPTER 78

Discipleship

*"By this my Father is glorified, that
you bear much fruit and so prove to
be my disciples." —* John 15:8

uthor Caroline Westerhoff says, *"Once we have some
glimmer of who Jesus is, we then will be confronted by
the implications of the life of discipleship."*[75] Jesus' invitation
to follow Him is certainly a confrontation to our comfortable,
convenient, self-centered lives. We are confronted by demands
such as:

- Lay down your life
- Forsake earthly relationships
- Let go of material things
- Suffer ridicule
- Bear fruit
- Be teachable
- Love your enemies
- Serve everyone

As mentioned earlier, Jesus said in John 8:31, "If you abide
in my word, you are truly my disciples." For Jesus to say *truly*
implies that there are disciples who are *not truly* disciples.

There are authentic and inauthentic disciples. Some talk the talk, others walk the walk. There is discipleship that is merely outward, and then there are disciples who are shaken to the core and different in every way.

In Luke 2, we are given a beautiful narrative of the birth and childhood of Jesus. Mary is pregnant. Jesus is born. He's circumcised. They have a baby dedication and then they flee to Egypt. The Bible fast-forwards to a 12-year-old Jesus in the Temple in Jerusalem. His parents got frustrated with him, because parents are naturally frustrated with preteens, right?. Then there's this one verse that sums up his life — from the hormonal pre-teen hanging out in the Temple to the young man on a mission to reach and redeem humanity through a brutal, inconceivable death on the cross. That verse is Luke 2:52 — "And Jesus grew in wisdom and stature, and in favor with God and man." He grew.

He grew in wisdom. Although He was fully divine, He grew in human intelligence. He gained new insights and learned new skills. He grew in stature. He got older, which means he got stronger and taller. His physical body matured. He grew in favor with God, experiencing the loving kindness and intimate Presence of the Father. And He grew in favor with man. He had a good reputation in the village and his relationships flourished. He was a good friend.

The Greek word in this verse translated as "grow" is taken literally to mean he "kept increasing and advancing." The challenge of discipleship is this: keep increasing and advancing. There is no scale that measures discipleship. There is no pace in which you must spiritually mature. There is no monthly submission of how many sins you committed. There's no box to check to confirm you're on your way to becoming a fully devoted disciple.

Just keep increasing.

Just keep advancing.

And find someone to help you increase and advance. Prayerfully find someone and invite him or her to disciple you (preferably, young ladies ask an older woman to disciple you; young men, ask an older man). Ask God to give you someone 20 or more years older than you are, someone who loves Jesus deeply, who has a good reputation in the community, a strong marriage, and a good understanding of God's Word. Meet regularly with this person throughout college (once each week if possible). Bring your questions to this person. Ask him or her to teach you more about the Father, Son, and Holy Spirit, more about the Bible, and more about discovering your gifts and purposes.

Every single moment that the disciples spent with Jesus, they were encouraged to increase and advance in their faith. So, sitting with someone who is far more mature and experienced in their faith life will do the same to you.

CHAPTER 79

Community

"Encourage one another and build up one another..." — 1 Thessalonians 5:11

Harvard Medical School conducted a study of adult development over a span of 75 years. Their research looked at the physical and mental health of two very different groups of people:

1. 268 Harvard University sophomores from the classes of 1939-1944.
2. 456 disadvantaged *(non-criminal)* inner-city boys from Boston.

All the subjects of this study were male and have American nationality. Those that are still alive are still being studied today, and the primary research includes: mental health, physical health, career enjoyment, marital quality, sex life, retirement experience, and the effects of combat (80% of the participants in this study served in World War II). The primary goal of this study was to identify predictors of healthy aging. George Vaillant, who directed the study for more than 30 years, published a summary statement: *"Warmth of relationships throughout life have the greatest positive impact on life satisfaction."*[76]

So, the most affluent, privileged, elite, upper-class university students shared the same results as the disadvantaged, at-risk youth from the inner city. This proves that all of humanity, no matter how different, has a common need: community. I guess this is why David (the baby of a lower class family and common shepherd) and Jonathan (the first born of a wealthy, royal family) became best friends (see 1 Samuel 18:3). In Part 7, I went into great detail on the importance of friendships, but you must know that your need for close community is uniquely designed by God.

Paul David Tripp says, *"True friendship calls you out of the darkness of personal privacy into the loving candor of mutual concern. It moves you from being a sealed envelope to an open letter."*[77] So much of the purpose of walking in community with others is that they hold you accountable to walk in the light. The more you walk in isolation, the more prone you are to secret sin. The more you secretly sin, the more prone you are to destruction.

Look at it this way:

The gospel = God is for us, despite us.

Friendship = Because of the gospel, I am for you, despite you.

Vulnerability = Admitting to someone, "I need you to be for me, despite me."

Find that someone, and begin walking in community, and don't wait until your senior year to prioritize Christian fellowship. The best time to find a Christian community to belong to is yesterday.

CHAPTER 80

Solitude

"But he would withdraw to desolate places and pray." — Luke 5:16

I'm intentionally writing about solitude on the heels of encouraging you to pursue community. Solitude is also incredibly important during your college years, and especially for you raging extroverts that can't stand 5 minutes of alone time.

Jesus is a great example and demonstrates the necessity of alone time by slipping away from the crowds. The call on His life was *for people,* but in order to handle people, He had to *get away from people!*

It is extremely easy (I know from experience) for all of your time with Jesus to include others (church, small group, retreats, etc.). That is important, but more important is that *you get to know Jesus personally.* David Benner writes, *"What God wants is simply our presence, even if it feels like a waste of potentially productive time. That is what friends do together — they waste time with each other. Simply being together is enough without expecting to 'get something' from the interaction. It should be no different with God."*[78]

Enjoying time with God doesn't have to be on your couch with a Bible, highlighter, a cup of coffee, and soothing music (the typical "quiet time" format). Instead, look for moments in which you can simply enjoy God's Presence, just the two of you.

CHAPTER 81

Trials

"Blessed is the man who remains steadfast under trial, for when he has stood the test he will receive the crown of life, which God has promised to those who love him." — James 1:12

If you lift weights, you probably know what makes your muscles go from big to bigger. They tear. Lifting weights tears your muscle fibers down, and when you follow a workout with a protein shake, the nutrients build back the tear and make the muscle stronger. This is what trials do with our lives. Neil Anderson shares, *"Trials and tribulations can actually be the catalyst for achieving God's goal for our lives, which is our sanctification."*[79] Trials help us become more holy.

As a college pastor, half of my meetings with students were conversations about trials. I met with students who were depressed, anxious, and suicidal. Students who were diagnosed with cancer, failing classes, or crippled by fear. Students who lost a parent or watched their parents walk through a nasty divorce. Students who were dumped by a girlfriend they were ready to marry and others who were sexually assaulted or raped. Students who were addicted to pornography, masturbation, drugs, alcohol, or gambling. Students who were simply disappointed that things weren't going their way.

First of all, God welcomes any of our emotions. He is not alarmed or disappointed if your situations lead you to pray prayers of frustration. He doesn't get mad at you if you get mad at Him. Trials are incredibly important to the development of our faith, and sadly, we live in a very broken, messy world. But, I suppose we can't truly know how much faith we have until it is put to the test.

Second, trials do not discriminate. No one is exempt. We are all victims. Good things have happened in your life because of how people around you have responded to their trials. And your testimony of enduring and overcoming trials can be positive for another person's life. Pain can be recycled and used for good.

In James 1:2-4, we read, "Consider it pure joy, my brothers and sisters, whenever you face trials of many kinds, and because you know the testing of your faith produces perseverance. Let perseverance finish its work so that you may be mature and complete, not lacking anything." A trial is a distress of any kind that will test and purify your Christian character. This is when wickedness, evil, or unexpected tragedy inconveniently pay you a visit. Trials can be relational, physical, emotional, mental, financial, spiritual, or vocational. When James says to consider it pure joy on the very worst of days, he's not saying to be joyful in the trial, but to be joyful in God's Presence and goodness through the trial. As a Christian, you don't have to act happy about cancer or abuse or car accidents. Those are still horrible. There is no obligation to slap on a fake smile and pretend that all is well. There is no pressure for you to fake it till you make it. That's ridiculous advice! Instead, face it till you make it. And you don't have to face it alone! You have the help of God, the encouragement of Scripture, the power of the Holy Spirit, and the fellowship of the Church!

The process of perseverance is not all that enjoyable. Back to

James: "we know" that we will grow as a result of our suffering. In the meantime, we remain steadfast, we have fortitude, we stand firm, and we trust the Lord.

At the end of the day, even after encouragement from Scripture and the support of family and friends, I remember students saying, *"I just can't handle this. I can't take this any longer. I don't care anymore. I wish I weren't even here. I wish I could just die."* In those darkest moments, zoom out of the trial and remember that God is sovereign. As someone once said, "Don't tell God how big your problems are. Tell your problems how big your God is!"

God does not wish chaos on your life. He does not want your distress to give birth to depression. He does not want your disappointments to result in doubt. He does not want your inconveniences to lead to insecurity. As you weather any storm and find yourself in any kind of battle, keep your eyes on Him. Life is fragile, indeed, but in the end, God is faithful.

You might be reading this and feeling pretty beat up by life. If you are currently in the trenches of an unbearable trial, I encourage you to talk to your parents and your pastor. Allow others to come alongside you and help you catch your breath. The greatest encouragement I can give you if you feel helpless or defeated is from 2 Corinthians 4:16-18 — *"Do not lose heart. Though outwardly we are wasting away, inwardly we are being renewed day by day. For our light and momentary troubles are achieving for us an eternal glory that far outweighs them all. So lets fix our eyes not on what is seen, but on what is unseen, since what is seen is temporary, but what is unseen is eternal."*

If you are at a breaking point and feel like you can't make it another day because of the trials you are facing, please reach out for help. Many times, young people who are tempted to "end it all" don't tell someone because they are ashamed. Don't be ashamed to talk with someone! Dear friend, please know that you are incredibly valuable, and prayer, therapy, and medication can still help. If you have any temptation to harm yourself at any point, please call the **National Suicide Prevention Lifeline: 1-800-273-8255.**

CHAPTER 82

Fear

"When I am afraid, I put my trust in you." — Psalm 56:3

When I was 8-years-old, my family went on a vacation. I'll never forget some of the strangest news from my mom: "today we're going to swim with sharks." Excuse me? Why would we ever do such a stupid thing? I think that's where my fear of sharks began. We only swam with nurse sharks that day, but nevertheless, they're in the shark family. That's enough to scar me for life. I was afraid.

A few years into our marriage, Andrea and I were out on her family's boat in Missouri. I had seen her brothers, Kyle and Aaron, wake board many times and do all sorts of tricks behind the boat. It looked effortless. Although I had only ever bass fished off of a boat, I was ready to give wakeboarding a try. My very first attempt was a success. But, I got too cocky and thought I could jump the wake. The next thing I remember was my ears ringing, the taste of my own blood, and the sound of my wife's scream. I passed out, and once we finally arrived to the dock, the EMTs concluded that I had lost too much blood and the situation was serious. The drive to the head trauma unit would have taken too long, so a helicopter was on its way.

It kind of ticks me off that I was unconscious the only time I've ever been on a helicopter. Andrea was afraid.

Why do I share those stories? Because fear is a natural reaction to scary stuff. It is ok to be afraid of large fish with razor sharp teeth that could rip your body apart. It is also ok to be afraid if your spouse is flown off in a chopper covered in his or her own blood. Some fears are totally rational. But still, one of the greatest weapons our enemy uses to steal our peace and joy is fear. He messes with all of us until the point that we are paralyzed with fear. Can you believe that the average high school student today has the same level of anxiety as the average psychiatric patient in the early 1950s?[80] This is a significant problem! God knows that we panic when we aren't in control, and we panic when we don't know what tomorrow holds. Our thoughts are constantly under attack; so let me combine some promises of God's help in a way that you can read when you are afraid. Bookmark this page so you can access these truths when you need them:

Read this out loud when you are fearful: *"The Lord is my refuge and my fortress, My God in whom I trust! For in the day of trouble, God will hide me; He will lift me up on a rock. He hides me in the secret place of His Presence and keeps me secretly in His shelter. He is my rock and my fortress. I have strong confidence in Him. The name of the Lord is a strong tower; I run into it and I'm safe. When I am helpless and in distress, He is my defense. He is a refuge from my storm and a shade from the heat. God is my strength and my stronghold. He is my rock and my deliverer. In Him I take refuge; He is my shield."*[81]

I think God wants us to be happy. He wants us to enjoy His Presence and His glory. He wants us to experience an awe-filled joy, an unexplainable peace, and to feel the depths of love. He wants us to appreciate his creation and enjoy the company of one another. He wants us to laugh. He wants our hearts to overflow with gratitude and erupt with praise. But we cannot fully do and experience these things when we are crippled and entangled and tied down by fear!

I love to hide and scare my kids *(ok, and my wife)*. I video it, too. It is hilarious. And if you think I'm mean, maybe you need to have a little more fun. While I'm being playful with my kids, Satan is not playing with you. He loves to scare you. My friend, if you are afraid of something in your life right now, or something that *could happen*, I want you to know that fear is a liar. Remember, our enemy's native language is nothing but lies. I want to encourage you: whatever you are facing, God is with you.

Do not be afraid.

CHAPTER 83

Jerusalem

"But you will receive power when the Holy Spirit has come upon you, and you will be my witnesses in Jerusalem and in all Judea and Samaria, and to the ends of the earth." — Acts 1:8

I recently learned of a man who invited his father into an exchange of letters to dialogue about the Christian faith. While the father was fully against Christian doctrine, he lovingly accepted his son's invitation without hesitation. After three years of writing and replying to over thirty letters, the father surrendered to Jesus. Their letters have been compiled to create a riveting book that I could barely put down. If you have a parent who doesn't support your Christian faith, I highly encourage you to read the letters written between Gregory and Edward Boyd.[82]

Acts 1:8 makes is perfectly clear that there is a geographic context of mission: *"But you will receive power when the Holy Spirit comes on you; and you will be my witnesses in Jerusalem, and in all Judea and Samaria, and to the ends of the earth."* Many Christians consider "missions" as a 10-14 day trip to Kenya to facilitate a children's program and serve food to the poor. Let me be clear: I am a huge advocate of short-term mission trips.

If they are executed correctly, participants are moved so deeply that they spend the rest of their lives committed to a missional lifestyle, giving their time and resources, and engaging in evangelism. However, if you fly to Kenya to tell someone about Jesus, but you don't share the gospel with anyone in your family or neighborhood, your understanding of missions is twisted. That's why I love the Boyd's story previously mentioned. A son shared his faith with his dad.

Your mission starts in your Jerusalem: your family, your classrooms, and your roommates. The very first priorities in your mission are the people you see every single day...the people who share your culture and your language. And trust me, you are not far from the poor and broken. You are not far from the sick and needy, and places where you can minister and help those suffering to injustice, and others who are living in total darkness. If your understanding of missions begins in your backyard, your perspective and opportunity to be missional are great. If your understanding of missions is only going to the ends of the Earth, your perspective and opportunity are small.

So, put this book down and go share the gospel with your neighbor. Seriously, the person *next door.*

CHAPTER 84

Church

"The righteous will flourish like a palm tree,
they will grow like a cedar of Lebanon; planted
in the house of the Lord, they will flourish in
the courts of our God." — Psalm 92:12-13

First of all, you need to attend a church in college. Churches have also creatively provided a variety of times to meet for worship, including Saturday nights (for those of you who don't care about college football). The decision of where you worship in college is a very important one. Let me offer a few suggestions of what you should research about a church before you put down roots:

o Pray and ask the Lord to give you clarity and discernment in choosing a church. Even if you walk away with nothing but positive observations, listen to God when choosing a church.

o Does the pastor preach the Bible, and does he or she do so accurately? Listen carefully during sermons and examine the preaching. If you hear the Word of God preached incorrectly, that is not the right church to attend.

o   All pastors use personal life stories as sermon illustrations, and that is perfectly normal and acceptable. However, if the sermon includes 3-4 personal stories every single week, and you hear more about the pastor's life than the life of Jesus, you might want to find a different church with a pastor who exalts the Lord, and not himself or herself.

o   Avoid churches that speak comparatively about other churches.

o   Check out the church's vision and mission statement on their website. Are they statements you can support and align with?

o   Look into the church's denomination and doctrine.

o   Tithing is a biblical principal and important to practice. However, attend a church that encourages financial generosity and obedience without making you feel obligated to give, and guilty if you don't.

o   Confirm that the church is committed to the sacraments of baptism and the Eucharist (communion).

o   Consider other elements that are important to you: worship style, multi-generational, traditional vs. modern, diversity, emphasis on mission, etc.

Once you find a church to attend during your college years, put down some roots and be planted there. You aren't always going to agree with everything you see at any church, but the last thing the body of Christ needs is another young person hopping from church to church. Most church-hoppers have two things in common:

1.   Church-hoppers are chronic complainers. No matter where they attend, they're looking for something wrong and something to critique. These people like to complain

about problems and don't contribute to any solutions. They tell the pastor how to pastor and tell the worship leader how to lead worship. I've met some of these people during my years in ministry, and their feedback isn't constructive and helpful, but instead, belittling and harsh. Some of them are mean enough to be considered bullies. Complainers can definitely irritate pastors with their constant nagging and demeaning of the church. Much worse, though, is that the Church is the Bride of Christ. The last thing we ought to be slamming with our negativity is something so dear to our Savior.

2. Church-hoppers think that church is all about them. Church is not about us — the purpose of the Church is to glorify the Lord. When you attend church, it isn't because the worship, teaching, seat arrangements, room temperature, service times, and parking spaces are all conveniently centered on your preferences. You attend church to glorify God and let Him minister to your heart in order to mold and shape you to look more like Him. He likely won't fill you up if you're already full of yourself.

Ultimately, the people I've described above are consumers, not contributors. They spend more energy sharing their critiques with pastors than sharing their testimony with their neighbors. There are too many reasons to praise God to get caught up in complaining and consumerism.

Prayerfully find your church.

Don't hop around. Put down roots.

Then, open your heart and contribute something.

PART NINE

TEN YEARS FROM NOW

I graduated high school with a good enough GPA to get a scholarship. I made some very close friends, learned a little Spanish, won a state championship in basketball, and hated algebra. My senior year, I was invited to join the track team and competed for a state championship in the 4 x 800 (we got slaughtered). Also, I was crowned Prom King (and just typing that makes me laugh out loud).

I tied a bow on high school and sailed off into the ocean of uncertainty called college. And 4.5 years later, I tied a bow on college and sailed off into the ocean of uncertainty called 45 hours of work per week.

I'm 36-years-old as I write this. This probably won't shock you, but I never wear my championship ring, "Prom King" is not on my resume, and in my job, I never use systems of linear equations and inequalities or first-degree polynomials (algebra). As for my closest friends in high school, I still talk to *a few of them.*

As you transition from high school to college, and then college into the "real world," the things that matter to you the most will change. The most difficult moments you've experienced will be trumped by more difficult moments. In the same light, the great moments you've had won't compare to the even greater moments that are coming.

The day will then come when you begin to experience a phenomenon that hits all of us at some point. You've probably heard your parents say it every once in a while: *"time flies."* I'm not sure how it does, but yesterday, I was sitting in Dale Hall taking my first college exam at the University of Oklahoma. And today, I'm married with four children, a dog, a job, a mortgage, and a car payment.

Where did the time go? Please tell me if you know.

FYI, you'll be asking that question when you're 36-years-old, too. Where did the time go? Since it seems to inevitably disappear, the more intentional you are with your time, the better. You're going to blink in college, and when you open your eyes, you'll be in your mid-thirties. So, let me offer some things you can do now to help the future version of yourself. The following chapters are not rocket science. They won't fascinate you by any means. They are simple and practical ideas that I wish someone had told me.

CHAPTER 85

Networking

"If you want to go fast, go alone. If you want to go far, go with others." — African Proverb

On September 11, 2001, our nation was awakened to the reality of terrorism as 2,996 precious people perished and over 6,000 were seriously injured. In the hours following the attack on the World Trade Centers, something extraordinary happened. All modes of transportation out of Manhattan were shut down — subways, tunnels, and bridges. People fled to the shoreline of the Hudson River, hoping to escape by boat.

The U.S. Coast Guard had sent a message over the radio: *"All available boats, this is the Ice Age Coast Guard. Anyone willing to help with the evacuation of lower Manhattan, report to Pier 25 immediately."* Within 20 minutes, boats filled the horizon. One captain shared, *"If it floated, and it could get there, it got there."* Captain Vincent Andolino shared in an interview: *"I can't stand by and watch other people suffer. The only good part of that day was that everyone helped."*

This boat rescue wasn't planned. It wasn't rehearsed. These captains had no training. They just did what was needed. That day, Andolino and hundreds of other small boat captains contributed to the largest sea evacuation in history. It was much larger than that of World War II, where 339,000 British and

French soldiers were rescued from Dunkirk over the course of 9 days. On September 11, nearly 500,000 civilians were rescued by boat, and *it took less than 9 hours.*[83]

This is a classic example of "strength in numbers." But it also shows how we can accomplish more when we work together. The 9/11 Boat Lift was successful because of a network. You're going to quickly learn that your success throughout life will be considerably linked to your network. *Who you know is equally as important as what you know.* Actually, it might be more important.

I'm not encouraging you to be an inauthentic and over-the-top annoying schmoozer. But throughout college, start networking. Find others who share your interests. Remember people's names. Get people's phone numbers and email addresses and save them as a contact in your phone. Pay very close attention to those that you meet in college. You never know if one day down the road, they'll be helpful to you, or you could be helpful to them.

CHAPTER 86

Social Media

"Don't put anything online that you wouldn't want plastered on a billboard." — Erin Bury

Social media can be a great resource and make a positive impact. It can also cause you great trouble if you're not careful. Everything you post, share, or like online, as well as whom you follow, gives the world a decent idea of what your values are. Also, sarcasm is often interpreted incorrectly online, leaving people confused or angry. Then, there are the wars that people have sitting behind their computer screen. I have found that people will type in a much more aggressive way than they would ever talk face to face.

I once posted a question about hunting on Facebook. Dozens of comments later, someone concluded that I do not respect God's creation, as those poor animals are just living in their homes trying to survive. One woman said my comment was *nauseating* to her. Of course, someone always makes the spiritual turn: *how can you be a preacher and a hunter?* All that to say, whatever you post online will immediately reel in support from likeminded people, while simultaneously invite an argument from those who disagree with you. From my experience, it simply isn't wise to pick a fight online.

More than the drama that our posts can create is the fact that our posts never go away. Whatever you put online now can be searched for and found years later. According to a *Career Builder* Survey, 70% of employers use social media sites to research job candidates during the hiring process and 57% admit to not hiring a candidate because of content they've posted. Once hired, close to half of employers monitor their employee's social media sites and 34% of employers have reprimanded or fired an employee based on content found online.[84]

The same survey encourages you to be cautious posting provocative or inappropriate photographs, videos or information, photos including alcohol or drugs, or discriminatory comments related to race, gender, religion, sexuality, or political opinions. I've known plenty of college graduates who have struggled to find employment. Even with a great personality, people skills, a strong work ethic, and an impressive degree, the economy is not always kind to job-hunters. There are enough hurdles to jump to secure your career — don't complicate the process by posting ignorant, immature, embarrassing comments or images on your social media.

CHAPTER 87

Your (Pre)-Resume

"Be so good they can't ignore you." — Steve Martin

Too often, a senior in college starts crafting his or her resume and has a difficult time knowing what to include. There are a lot of outstanding resources online to help you write your resume, but I encourage you to start a "pre-resume" as soon as possible.

Open a Word document on your computer and title it "pre-resume." Write down everything you accomplished in high school. Think: GPA, job experience, clubs, teams, awards, certificates, volunteer experience, leadership positions, notable skills, relevant coursework that aligns with your degree or career interests… anything else that sounds remotely impressive and noteworthy. Then, add to that document at the end of each semester of college. When you graduate college, you won't have to remember everything you've accomplished or participated in because you'll have it all written down! This pre-resume will provide information to start your official resume, which you'll submit to potential employers.

While I encourage humility in every arena of your life, this pre-resume is different. When I look at a young person's resume, I want to see a confident assessment of what he or she has accomplished and is capable of. It might feel a little bit like bragging, but your resume is the one place that bragging is acceptable!

Along with what you type on your resume one day, you'll need to provide references — real life people who an employer can call and ask questions about your character and competence. Just to be clear, your references can't be your grandmother and best friend. Instead, pay close attention to your relationships throughout college with managers, supervisors, directors, professors, and any other authority figures or leaders who could one day serve as a reference.

Along with your birth certificate, social security card, high school diploma, college degree, and marriage license, your resume will always be one of the most important pieces of paper throughout your life. Just be sure you've worked hard enough to have something worthwhile to write on it!

CHAPTER 88

Job Interviews

*"Job hunting, applications, and interviews
are so fun!"* — Said No One Ever

I started working at a church part time when I was a senior in college. Upon graduating, I was offered a full time position on the church's staff. I already had relational equity and favor with the senior and executive pastors, so they didn't feel an interview was necessary. *They already knew me.* I suppose that's a compliment to the work I had done when I was a part-time employee, but in hindsight, I wish I got to experience the formal interview process.

Twelve years later, at 33-years-old, I was interviewed for the very first time. It was in a conference room with the senior pastor and leadership team of a church. I was nervous; it felt like something I should have already done a few times in my life. Nevertheless, I guess I did ok because they offered me the job. However, I have never had any formal training on how to interview well. I suppose my passion for Jesus and the Church was evident, but otherwise, I'm not sure I did much more to impress the team interviewing me.

The interview process is something you should read about and study before you graduate college. My father-in-law is the CEO of large company in Chicago that employs *a lot* of people. He shared with me that within 30 seconds, he has an opinion (positive or not) and the person has the remainder of the interview to change his mind. Usually the knock-out blow, he shared, is lack of preparation.

If leaders are impressed with your resume, you're just getting started. An invitation to interview allows them to look beyond what you put on paper. They'll notice your nonverbal communication and how you dressed. Do you listen well or talk too much? Do you act like an "expert" and come across too cocky? Or do you come across so humble that they wonder if you have any confidence at all. Are you a smooth talker or do you fumble your words? Do you come across genuinely interested in the job or just desperate for employment? Are you on time (which is 15 minutes early)? Have you researched the company already and prepared to ask relevant questions?

All that to say, don't depend solely on your charisma or impressive resume. At some point in college, practice interviewing with a roommate or friend. One of the greatest hires I've ever made in ministry simply didn't interview well the first time around (I told him this, and he agreed). I worked with him on his ability to coherently and concisely answer our questions and convey his passion with humble confidence. I called him back to our church for a second interview, and he hit the ball out of the park. Grand slam. He joined our staff three weeks later.

Case in point: interviews matter. So put in some research and practice prior to graduation so you are ready to go.

CHAPTER 89

Dream Big

*"When I grow up, I'm going to own a
snow cone stand."* — Macy Barnett

There was once a group of soldiers who had just been trained for their first parachute jump. Over and over again, they were told the steps to take in order to ensure their safety. Their sergeant reminded them what to do if their main chute did not open: *"Snap back immediately into position as we've taught you, and then pull the rip cord of your reserve chute, and it will open, bringing you safely to the ground."*

One soldier nervously asked, *"Sergeant, if my main parachute doesn't open, how long do I have to pull my reserve chute?"* The sergeant looked directly into the young soldier's eyes and earnestly replied, *"The rest of your life, soldier."*[85]

You know how long you have to pursue your dreams? *The rest of your life.*

I may not know you, but I know you have dreams. You have ambitions and goals. You have something that nags you in a good way and begs for your time, attention and energy. Every person who has significantly impacted the course of history started a movement with one simple idea. *A dream.*

Whatever your dreams are, pursue them! Go for it! There is so much this life has to offer you, and so much you have to offer to the world. The only problem is that we don't know when our lives will expire, so what are you waiting for? You better get started! Turn your dreams into reality!

CHAPTER 90

Two Tough Questions

"Fear not that thy life shall come to an end, but rather fear that it shall never have a beginning." — John Newman

D o you remember the first chapter of this book? I'm going to finish this thing the same way that I started it — with the same two questions:

1. Who are you becoming?
2. Do you like who you are becoming?

I'm not assuming that you've read the last 89 chapters and suddenly know who you are becoming or like who you are becoming. The point that I want to make here at the end of this book is this: you need to ask yourself those two questions the rest of your life. Ten years from now, you'll still be in the process of becoming more of the person you want to be. You'll still be growing and learning and messing things up and trying again.

I was recently with a friend who made some seriously terrible and destructive choices that almost wrecked his family. We had a conversation about these two questions. He wasn't happy whatsoever with the person he was becoming, and once he could admit it, he could make necessary changes and hit reset. His "reset button" was putting Jesus at the center of his life again. Things are in order again, and these questions, as well as an honest scan of his heart, seem to have saved his marriage (and maybe his life).

By God's design, you'll never *arrive* to the best version of you.

The finish line isn't here on earth.

So keep running. Keep becoming.

Occasionally make sure you like who you are becoming.

And remember, the ultimate aim and purpose of your life is to glorify God — today, ten years from now, and until your days on earth are finished. He is worthy of the glory and He has already accomplished most of the work on your behalf:

- He became sin so that you could become righteousness.
- He became a curse so that you could become redeemed.
- He became poor so that you might become rich.

Ultimately, *Jesus became* _____ *so you could become* _____.

To Him be the glory!

Thank you for allowing me to come with you on this journey called *college*. May God be with you and may God bless you!

APPENDIX A

When to Ask for Help

By Andrea Barnett

Asking for help is one of the greatest gifts we can give ourselves. God didn't create us to carry our burdens alone. Throughout our lifetime we will find ourselves in many situations where we need the support of others.

I've told college girls I've met with and mentored over the years that your season of college really is one of the hardest phases of life you'll face. While nearly everyone endures emotional or relational struggles at some point, many in college will experience other struggles, such as an eating disorder, abuse of alcohol, drugs or medication, pre-martial sex, homosexual thoughts, rape or sexual assault, an abusive relationship, or addition to pornography.

These struggles, and any others unmentioned, don't define you. Yet, still, many young people remain quiet out of fear of shame or embarrassment. Friend, if you are aware of an overwhelming situation in your life, reach out for spiritual, medical, or psychological help and counsel! Asking for help is one of the key ingredients in your journey to find freedom!

Keeping secrets, burying your guilt, or sitting in denial will only increase your pain.

While struggles we face in life don't define, they do tell a story of God's redemption. You are not alone! God is with you! And He is the first person you should turn to when you need help. Father God is always near to you, no matter what is going on in your life. The Presence of God is always ready to wrap His loving arms around you, meet you in your pain, bring you peace and provide you with wisdom. After you turn to the Lord, turn to whomever you feel can support and help you with your journey to freedom. The following are a few suggestions of whom you can call or turn to in your time of need:

- If you are in immediate danger or risk: Dial 911
- National Sexual Assault Hotline: 1-800-656-4673
- Sex Addiction Hotline: 1-877-708-5338
- Substance Abuse Helpline: 1-800-662-HELP
- American Addiction Center: 1-866-247-9051
- Pregnant and Need Help (National Life Center): 1-800-848-LOVE
- Pregnancy Resource Center: 1-800-395-HELP
- National Alliance of Mental Illness: 1-800-950-6264
- National Suicide Prevention Lifeline: 1-800-273-8255
- National Eating Disorder Association Helpline: 1-800-931-2237
- Research local churches near your campus and meet a pastor
- Licensed Professional Counselor and/or Therapist

APPENDIX B

Recommended Reading

In my experience as a college pastor, one of the greatest ways to lead a student is to suggest books to read. The following are books that I have recommended over the years (after the Bible, of course) and they are in alphabetical order by the author's first name. While I believe these books offer helpful insights in a variety of topics, recommending them does not mean that I fully agree with each author doctrinally.

To learn how to grow in your faith: <u>Spiritual Discipline Handbook</u> by Adele Calhoun

To learn how to live with passion: <u>Live Life on Purpose</u> by Claude Hickman

To learn how to love recklessly: <u>Crazy Love</u> by Francis Chan

To learn about the Holy Spirit: <u>Forgotten God</u> by Francis Chan

To learn your personal style of love: <u>The Five Love Languages</u> by Gary Chapman

To learn the value of diversity: <u>Jesus and the Disinherited</u> by Howard Thurman

To learn the power of forgiveness: <u>Left to Tell</u> by Immaculee Illibigaza

To learn how to reach your potential: <u>Don't Waste Your Life</u> by John Piper

To learn how to defend your faith: <u>The Case for Christ</u> by Lee Strobel

To learn how answers to tough questions: <u>The Case for Faith</u> by Lee Strobel

To learn why these years matter: <u>The Defining Decade</u> by Meg Jay

To learn how to overcome sin: <u>Victory Over Darkness</u> by Neil Anderson

To learn how to lead with integrity: <u>Spiritual Leadership</u> by Oswald Sanders

To learn how to be a godly man: <u>The Masculine Mandate</u> by Richard Phillips

To learn your personality type: <u>The Enneagram</u> by Richard Rohr

To learn why you are here: <u>Purpose Driven Life</u> by Rick Warren

To learn how to steward finances: <u>The Blessed Life</u> by Robert Morris

To learn how to live with purpose: <u>Doing Things That Matter</u> by Tim Mannin

To learn God's design for sexuality: <u>Song of Solomon</u> by Tommy Nelson

APPENDIX C

What Former Students Are Saying

"I am honored to say that I have been able to hear the word of God from Adam since I was elementary age through my time in college. The way Adam is able to capture the attention and feed in to the hearts of students is nothing short of a gift from God. The way he leads is not as an authority figure, but as a TRUE friend. He gives you the truth whether it hurts or not. He has been there for me personally through the hardest time in my life and through the most eye opening, uplifting mission trip of my life. I am forever grateful to have this man in my life and call him a friend.

— Beau Proctor
Physical Therapist
(Oklahoma City, OK)

"Adam's life, as is demonstrated in his family and his ministry, is one continually marked by consistency and integrity. He has served to be the stable role model to several youth and college students in a generation marked by anxiety and individualism. He unashamedly believes and proclaims the truths of God's Word to be the solution to young people's challenges. It is clear from personal experience that Adam deeply cares about God's image-bearers. This is apparent by his truthful, yet longsuffering and gracious approach to the students he

has discipled over the years. Truly, there are few as qualified as Adam Barnett to effectively speak into the lives of young people."

— **Brandon Ehardt**
Middle School Teacher
(Hamilton, MA)

"Adam Barnett is not only someone I look up to personally, but is a trustworthy man of God to follow. Adam was able to impact my life at the perfect time. The Holy Spirit guided Adam in leading me to not just follow Christ, but to LIVE for Him. Now that I work with college students, I find myself doing and saying the same things Adam did and I hope that my son finds someone like him when he is in college. At the end of the day, Adam is engaged with what is going on with college students and knows how to influence and impact that generation, both to pursue Christ, and also to prepare them for life."

— **Brent Potter**
Assistant Director of Kanakuk KampOut
(Branson, MO)

"The influence that Adam has had on my life has helped me in so many areas. Adam has taught me so many valuable lessons on what it's like to walk boldly with the Lord on a daily basis. I am thankful that Adam was able to minister and guide me throughout my formidable years at OU, as he taught me that even though I may go through trials, I am always able to rely on Christ, as He is my rock and foundation no matter what may happen. I know I can always reach out to him for anything, especially with the challenges I face being in the NBA everyday. I'm glad I have someone like Adam as a spiritual role model in my life."

— **Buddy Hield**
Sacramento Kings Shooting Guard
(Sacramento, CA)

"Adam's influence helped me become closer to Christ. I told Adam I wanted to be baptized while we were in Haiti, and he asked me a

question I'll never forget: 'are you doing this because of the moment, or because you mean it?' His question showed me that Adam is intentional in his ministry. I'm thankful for all Adam has done for me spiritually and emotionally."

— **Cody Ford**
Buffalo Bills Offensive Lineman
(Buffalo, NY)

"I am thankful for Adam's guidance. He was there for me during the good and bad times of my college career. He is an inspiration to me, teaching me to be great in this life and that I can change the lives of those around me by just being myself. His influence in my life, most importantly, brought me closer to Jesus Christ. I appreciate all he's done!"

— **Corey Nelson**
Tampa Bay Buccaneers Linebacker
2016 Super Bowl 50 Champion
(Tampa, FL)

"Adam's ability to connect with and shepherd young people is truly something special. He is a strong leader while being transparent and endlessly genuine; a rare combo in today's world. He is a master encourager and promotes the gifts and talents of others, which empowers them to find and walk in the calling that God has placed on their lives. I've personally been blessed by Adam's friendship, his leadership, and being under his watch during my college years. If you're heading into college, I would highly recommend you read this book and take it to heart. He won't steer you wrong!

— **Jonathan McQuitty**
Worship Director
(Lakewood, FL)

"I trust Adam Barnett with my life. As a mentor, he saw the ugliness of my sin exposed and like a skilled surgeon, he confronted it while maintaining the dignity and respect every young man's heart craves.

259

He has coached me through some of the biggest and hardest lessons I've ever had to learn. I love my big bro. I trust that you will, too."

— Joshua Burr
Oklahoma National Guard, 63rd CST WMD
(Norman, OK)

"Adam Barnett is a man I have said many times that I would follow to the ends of the earth. No one person has had more of an impact on my life, my relationship with Jesus, and the way I lead my students than Adam has. Since meeting him my freshman year of college, Adam has encouraged, challenged, corrected and mentored me with authentic love, grace and truth to live a Christ-centered life in community with other believers. I am truly blessed to not only call him my mentor, but also my dear friend. Adam consistently lives his life as a Christlike example and any student would be better for patterning their life after his example and teaching."

— Josiah Barkley
Middle School Ministry Director
(Tulsa, OK)

"We are so thankful for the influence Adam has had in our lives. He walked with us through college and led us from there into marriage with great wisdom. He is our trusted resource of Godly counsel and we have grown significantly in our faith because of our time learning from him."

— Kevin and Veronica Burns
Meteorologist and Interior Designer
(St. Petersburg, FL)

"My relationship with Adam began at such a critical time in my life. As a new believer in high school with my father on a different continent and my mother working three jobs, his example, counsel, and leadership helped shape me into the man I am today. It his investment into my spirit, my character, and my knowledge of the Gospel of Christ throughout high

school and college that lay a foundation of faith, hope, and humility in Jesus for both my life and my marriage."

— **Khalil Benalioulhaj**
Benali Marketing
(Norman, OK)

"Adam was a gift when I was going through college. He conveyed the messages of the Bible in such a relatable and revealing way. College challenges can be new and plentiful, and I felt that I could come to him and his family at any time with anything. He actively found ways to help me combat my anxieties and give me plans of action through God's Word and his own experiences."

— **Lauren Chamberlain**
Professional Softball Player
(Edmond, OK)

"If there were a time in my life where I could go back, it would be during my college years. The reason I would go back is to listen, watch, and take more notes from my college mentor, Adam. I've realized that his teaching not only taught me about how to be a man, but the lessons I learned have been applicable for my marriage, and now parenthood. He's wise beyond his years and his teaching applies timeless truths."

— **Michael Hewett**
Young Life Area Director
(Coppell, TX)

"College is a time of incredible self discovery. All of a sudden, you are responsible for deciding what and who will and won't be a part of your life, what you do and don't stand for, who you are and who you want to become. When I walked through those decisions, Pastor Adam's teaching, encouragement, and friendship were an absolute game changer for me. While Pastor Adam was able to speak to the specific difficulties that came with that age, he was also able to inspire me, and countless others, to simply treasure the gospel above all else. I *can't speak highly enough of Pastor Adam's character, his pure love for Jesus, and the anointing on his life to help young people authentically know, love, and serve God."*

— **Powell Benalioulhaj**
Benali Marketing
(Norman, OK)

"Adam has mentored more college students than I'll ever know, and he still managed to walk with me side-by-side as I embarked on the tough-yet-rewarding journey of walking with the Lord in college. Adam is one of the few men in my life that have directly impacted my life as a husband, father and friend. No one is more qualified or experienced in understanding the challenges facing college students today, and how to embrace them as a Christian. I have known Adam for 15 years and consider him a brother and mentor, and trust his leadership of college-aged students will shine through his words in this book."

— **Riley Cummins**
Small Business Owner/Real Estate
(Santa Rosa Beach, FL)

"Adam Barnet is a real winner. He has a heart for leadership. He has taken it upon himself to learn the word of God and to share it with the world. I can speak of that from my personal experience. Adam came into my life in college and led me to rededicate my life to Christ. He did this not by only standing on the podium, but having a real life, one-on-one relationship with me. He mentored me on a weekly basis helping me grow more spiritually. Adam's leadership was a big part of my daily transformation. He made such an enormous impact on my life."

— **Ryan Broyles**
Entrepreneur
(Norman, OK)

"A man of God, pastor, mentor, best friend, confidence builder, advice giver... Anything you need, he is there for. When I started college at OU, I was lost and had to figure it out. Adam was there to not only

get me closer to our Savior, but to mentor me through school and basketball seasons. When I played professional basketball in Japan, guess who met with me on Facetime and walked me through the Bible? Adam Barnett. I cannot say enough about this man and what he has meant to me."

— **Ryan Spangler**
Sales Manager
(Oklahoma City, OK)

"'Lets Be Honest… Are you Really Ready for College?' is an outstanding source for young adults looking for insights on how to smoothly make the transition from high school to college. It doesn't have all the answers — no one has all the answers, and no one ever will, but the detail Adam gives in each chapter allows the reader to connect on an almost personal level to him and his testimony."

— **Samaje Perine**
Washington Redskins Running Back
(Ashburn, VA)

"I was fortunate enough to first get to know Adam as the leader of our annual 'Sooners 4 Haiti' mission trip, taken each year by a group of Oklahoma student-athletes. In a short period of time thereafter, Adam became one of the most important figures in my walk with Christ, meeting weekly to walk through the ups and downs that life inevitably presents. Adam has incredible experience as a high school and college pastor and I would consider him one of the strongest men of faith that I know. His ability to relate to any and all types of people is truly a spiritual gift. Adam's dedication to the Gospel gives me pure confidence the contents of this book will change countless lives because it is written by an ultimate spiritual warrior."

— **Trevor Knight**
Financial Services
(Dallas, TX)

"Adam was the single most influential person in my life and my courtship of my wife. God has personally blessed me with the opportunity to be discipled by Adam and join him on mission trips. He has a mixture of unapologetic, bold, biblical preaching and Spirit-filled charisma. I always admire someone who is willing to risk success for teaching hard truths, and Adam always did that in a humble manner, as he is submitted to the Word of God."

— Trey Millard
Field Engineer
(Norman, OK)

"As a freshman in college over a thousand miles from home, I turned to Adam for much-needed mentorship and guidance. Looking back now, I cannot begin to estimate his impact on my life. He is a wise counselor, a humble servant, and an incredible friend! I am forever grateful for his investment in my life!"

— Ty Darlington
University of Oklahoma Football Coach
(Norman, OK)

"Adam Barnett has a unique gift to recognize potential in students and breathe encouragement that meets them where they are, but leads them to where God has called. His influence in our college years impacted each of our personal relationships with Jesus, and in doing so, has truly shaped the foundation of our marriage, and now family. The weight that his words carry is significant, and our respect for Adam has been earned through many years of us witnessing his relentless pursuit God!"

— Tyler and Kristin Neal
Benali Marketing
(Oklahoma City, OK)

APPENDIX D

About The Author

Photo by: @sarahjanesphotography

Adam Barnett lives in Tulsa, Oklahoma with his wife, Andrea, and their four children: Macy, André, Ellie, and Gracía. He is a graduate of the University of Oklahoma and North Park Theological Seminary. Adam currently serves as one of the pastors at Redeemer Church.

Adam has been in vocational ministry since 2005, including years as a Junior-High Pastor, High School Pastor, and College Pastor. Additionally, he developed an internship program that has launched countless students into various ministry positions across the country.

Along with student and college ministry, Adam's experience includes various speaking engagements, local and international missions, travel to 50 countries, leadership development and training, and leading over ten different teams of collegiate and professional athletes to serve in Haiti.

Interact with Adam on social media: @AdamLBarnett.

Email **questions** or **prayer requests**: hello@adambarnett.org.

Book Adam to **speak at your church or event** at adambarnett.org.

END NOTES

Part One:

1   Meg Jay, *The Defining Decade* (New York, NY: Hachette Book Group, 2012), xxxi.
2   Klyne Snodgrass, *Who God Says You Are* (Grand Rapids, MI: Eerdman's Publishing Group, 2018), 12.
3   Tim Mannin, *Doing Things That Matter* (Oklahoma City, OK: Uptown Publishing, 2017), 47.
4   John Piper, *Don't Waste Your Life* (Wheaton, IL: Crossway Books, 2003), 48.
5   Mannin, 57.
6   1947 September, The Reader's Digest, Volume 51, (Filler item), Quote Page 64, The Reader's Digest Association.
7   That's not really my math, but a combination of research. I don't even understand the equation.
8   All of these stories and many others can be found at https://www.wanderlustworker.com/48-famous-failures-who-will-inspire-you-to-achieve/.
9   *Oxford Dictionary of Quotations (3rd edition).* Oxford University Press. 1979. p. 251.
10 "Statistics about Teenagers and Self Worth," Stage of Life, February 2015, www.stageoflife.com/StageHighSchool/Statistics_on_High_School_Students_and_Teenagers.aspx.
11 "The Water Crisis," water.org, Accessed May 1, 2019, https://water.org/our-impact/water-crisis/.

Part Two:

12 Sanders, Oswald J. *Spiritual Leadership* (Chicago, IL: Moody Press, 1967), 94.

13 Luffey Haberman, *"Weighing in College Students Diet and Exercise Behaviors"* (January 1998, 189-191), https://www.tandfonline.com/doi/abs/10.1080/07448489809595610.

Part Three:

14 "Beginning College Students Who Change Their Majors Within 3 Years of Enrollment," Data Point, Accessed May 10, 2019, https://nces.ed.gov/pubs2018/2018434.pdf.

15 National Longitudinal Surveys, Bureau of Labor Statistics, Accessed May 11, 2019, https://www.bls.gov/nls/nlsfaqs.htm.

16 Sanders, Oswald J. *Spiritual Leadership* (Chicago, IL: Moody Press, 1967), 98.

17 Westerhoff, Caroline. *Calling: A Song for the Baptized* (New York, NY: Church Publishing, 2005), 35.

18 "Honor System Rules," Texas A & M University, Accessed May 15, 2019, https://aggiehonor.tamu.edu/Rules-and-Procedures/Rules/Honor-System-Rules.

Part Four:

19 Howard L. Dayton, Jr., "Jesus' Teachings on Money," Preaching Today, Accessed May 25, 2019, https://www.preachingtoday.com/illustrations/1996/december/410.html.

20 James Patterson, *The Day America Told the Truth* (New Jersey: Prentice Hall Trade, 1991), 65.

21 The following are professionals who can help train you to budget your finances, and many of their resources are free: Financial Peace University (daveramsey.com); Personal Finance for College Students (incharge.org); What is Money? (practicalmoneyskills.com); Budget for College Student's Spending (nerdwallet.com).

22 Alex Glenn, "Cost of Raising a Child," Nerd Wallett, March 20, 2017, https://www.nerdwallet.com/blog/insurance/cost-of-raising-a-child/.

23   Elizabeth Hoyt, "Over 2.9 Billion in Free College Money Unclaimed by Students – Why?" January 20, 2015, https://www.fastweb.com/financial-aid/articles/over-2-point-nine-billion-in-free-college-money-unclaimed-by-students-why.

24   Nace Staff, "Class of 2018's Preliminary Starting Salary Shows Slight Drop, October 10, 2018, https://www.naceweb.org/job-market/compensation/class-of-2018s-preliminary-starting-salary-shows-slight-drop/.

25   "Am I Rich?" Remember the Poor, Accessed June 2, 2019, https://irememberthepoor.org/3-2/.

26   Piper, 102.

27   Piper, 72.

28   Piper, 45-46.

Part Five:

29   Eugene Peterson, *The Message* (Colorado Springs: NavPress Publishing Group, 2003), 1,674-1,675.

30   Eric & Leslie Ludy, *Teaching True Love to a Sex-at-13 Generation* (Nashville: Thomas Nelson, 2005), 109-110.

31   "STDs in Adolescents and Young Adults," Center for Disease Control and Prevention, Accessed May 25, 2019, https://www.cdc.gov/std/stats17/adolescents.htm.

32   Paola Bailey, "Sexual Assault on College Campuses," May 27, 2017, https://blog.paolabailey.com/sexual-assault-on-college-campuses-4117be4e3b0d.

33   "11 Facts About Human Trafficking," Do Something, Accessed May 25, 2019, https://www.dosomething.org/us/facts/11-facts-about-human-trafficking.

34   B. Sims, "Get Your Mind Right: A Little Porn Never Hurt Anybody, June 14, 2007, https://hiphopdx.com/editorials/id.793/title.get-your-mind-right-a-little-porn-never-hurt-anybody#.

35   Sheryl Kraft, "6 Theories Why Men Cheat," September 15, 2015, https://www.healthywomen.org/content/article/6-theories-why-men-cheat.

36   Wendy Tuohy, "Rougher, Harder, Violent: How Porn is Warping the Male Mind," July 23, 2015, https://www.dailytelegraph.com.au/rendezview/rougher-harder-violent-how-porn-is-warping-the-male-mind/newsstory/504698ce318f551052847f13ac678fd1.

37 There are many ways you can get help: Call the Sex Addiction Hotline (800-477-8191), see a local therapist, visit a local pastor for advice on getting help, or email me for other resources.

38 Meg Meeker, *Strong Fathers, Strong Daughters: 10 Secrets Every Father Should Know* (New York: Ballantine, 2007), 20.

39 "How Effective Are Condoms?" Accessed May 28, 2019, https://www.plannedparenthood.org/learn/birth-control/condom/how-effective-are-condoms.

40 Meeker, 20.

41 Ludy, 79.

42 Sara G. Miller, "Why Sexual Assault Victims Wait to Speak Out," October 9, 2017, https://www.livescience.com/56482-victims-sexual-assault-speak-out.html.

43 Sara G. Miller, "5 Misconceptions About Sexual Assault," October 13, 2016, https://www.livescience.com/56480-misconceptions-about-sexual-assault.html.

44 Wiki Media Commons, Accessed June 5, 2019, https://commons.wikimedia.org/wiki/File:Sea_turtle_nest_sign_(Boca_raton,_FL).jpg.

45 U.S Fish and Wildlife Service, "Federal Laws That Protect Bald Eagles," March 4, 2019, https://www.fws.gov/midwest/eagle/protect/laws.html.

46 "State Homicide Laws That Recognize Unborn Victims," National Right to Life, April 2, 2018, https://www.nrlc.org/federal/unbornvictims/statehomicidelaws092302/.

47 One great example of those willing to help can be found at http://ababystepadoption.com.

Part Six:

48 National Highway Traffic Safety Administration, "Traffic Safety Facts 2016: Alcohol Impaired Driving, October 2017, https://crashstats.nhtsa.dot.gov/Api/Public/ViewPublication/812450.

49 National Institute on Alcohol Abuse and Alcoholism, "Alcohol Facts and Statistics," June, 2017, https://www.niaaa.nih.gov/alcohol-health/overview-alcohol-consumption/alcohol-facts-and-statistics.

50 Bernstein, Larry. *Alcohol Poisoning* (The Washington Post, January 6, 2015).

51 MADD, "Statistics," December 31, 2017, https://www.madd.org/statistics/.

52   Centers for Disease Control and Prevention, "Fact Sheets – Excessive Alcohol Use and Risks to Women's Health, March 7, 2016, https://www.cdc.gov/alcohol/fact-sheets/womens-health.htm.

53   Centers for Disease Control and Prevention "Fact Sheets – Excessive Alcohol Use and Risks to Women's Health, March 7, 2016, https://www.cdc.gov/alcohol/fact-sheets/womens-health.htm.

54   Hingson, R.W.; Zha, W.; Weitzman, E.R. Magnitude of and trends in alcohol-related mortality and morbidity among U.S. college students ages 18–24, 1998–2005. *Journal of Studies on Alcohol and Drugs* (Suppl. 16):12–20, 2009.

55   Hingson, R.; Heeren, T.; Winter, M.; et al. Magnitude of alcohol-related mortality and morbidity among U.S. college students ages 18–24: Changes from 1998 to 2001. *Annual Review of Public Health* 26:259–279, 2005.

56   Wechsler, H.; Dowdall, G.W.; Maenner, G.; et al. Changes in binge drinking and related problems among American college students between 1993 and 1997: Results of the Harvard School of Public Health College Alcohol Study. *Journal of American College Health* 47(2):57–68, 1998.

57   The Addiction Center, "The Relationship Between Alcohol and Crime," Accessed June 10, 2019, https://www.addictioncenter.com/alcohol/alcohol-related-crime/.

58   National Highway Traffic Safety Administration. "The Economic and Societal Impact Of Motor Vehicle Crashes, 2010." National Highway Traffic Safety Administration, May 2014, DOT HS 812 013. http://www-nrd.nhtsa.dot.gov/Pubs/812013.pdf.

59   U.S. Department of Transportation, "2017 Fatal Motor Vehicle Crashes: Overview," October, 2018, https://crashstats.nhtsa.dot.gov/Api/Public/ViewPublication/812603.

60   Center on Addiction, "Know the Facts: Addiction is a Disease," Accessed June 16, 2019, https://www.centeronaddiction.org/addiction.

61   Center on Addiction, "Know the Facts: Addiction is a Disease," Accessed June 16, 2019, https://www.centeronaddiction.org/addiction.

Part Seven:

62   Maxie Dunnam, *The Preachers Commentary* (Nashville: Thomas Nelson, 1982), vol. 31, p. 275.

63 Eugene Peterson, *The Message Bible* (Colorado Springs: NavPress Publishing, 2003), 1,727.

64 A. Psychologists at Harvard, the University of Virginia and the University of Washington created "Project Implicit," (implicit. harvard.edu/implicit/takeatest.html) which measures unconscious biases. B) The Intercultural Development Inventory: idiinventory.com. C) To browse books that explain cultural patterns and differences: interculturalpress.com.

65 Jonathan Pennington, *The Sermon on the Mount and Human Flourishing* (Grand Rapids: Baker Academic, 2017), 266.

66 Joseph Grenny, Ron McMillan, Kerry Patterson and Al Switzler. *Crucial Conversations: Tools for Talking when Stakes are High* (New York, NY: McGraw Hill, 2012), 9.

67 Joseph, McMillan, Patterson and Switzler, 3.

68 Immaculée Ilibagiza, *Left to Tell* (Carlsbad, CA: Hay House, Inc., 2006), 204.

Part Eight:

69 Foster, Richard. *Streams of Living Water* (New York, NY: Harper One Publishers, 1998), 85.

70 Westerhoff, Caroline. *Calling: A Song for the Baptized* (New York, NY: Church Publishing, 2005), 141.

71 McGrath, Alister. *Christian Theology: An Introduction* (Malden, MA: Blackwell, 2001), 325.

72 Zahl, Paul F. *Grace in Practice: A Theology of Everyday Life* (Grand Rapids, MI: Eerdmans, 2007), 36.

73 Sanders, Oswald J. *Spiritual Leadership* (Chicago, IL: Moody Press, 1967), 85.

74 Oswald Chambers, *Utmost Classic Readings and Prayers* (Grand Rapids: Oswald Chambers Publications Association, 2012), Day 58.

75 Westerhoff, 22.

76 Harvard Medical School, "The Grant Study," Accessed June 5, 2019, https://en.wikipedia.org/wiki/Grant_Study.

77 Paul David Tripp, *Instruments in the Redeemer's Hands* (Phillipsburg: P & R Publishing, 2002), 45.

78 Benner, David G. *The Gift of Being Yourself* (Downers Grove, IL: IVP Press, 2015), 39.

79 Anderson, Neil. *Victory Over The Darkness* (Ventura, CA: Regal Books, 2000), 134.

80 Clark, Taylor. *Nerve: Poise Under Pressure, Serenity Under Stress, and the Brave New Science of Fear and Cool* (New York, NY: Little and Brown, 2011), 11.

81 Psalm 91:2, 27:5, 31:20, 18:2 and 71:3; Proverbs 14:26, 18:10, Isaiah 25:4; Jeremiah 16:19.

82 Boyd, Gregory and Edward. *Letters from a Skeptic* (Colorado Springs, CO: David Cook, 2008).

Part Nine:

83 Road to Resilience, "BOATLIFE: An Untold Tale of 9/11 Resilience," September 7, 2011, https://www.youtube.com/watch?v=MDOrzF7B2Kg.

84 Career Builder, "More Than Half of Employers Have Found Content on Social Media That Caused Them NOT to Hire a Candidate, August 9, 2018, https://www.prnewswire.com/news-releases/.

85 The Reader's Digest (New York City: Random House Inc., February 1982).

CPSIA information can be obtained
at www.ICGtesting.com
Printed in the USA
BVHW041101141119
563830BV00014B/1745/P